A PLUME BOOK

You Buy the Peanut Butter, I'll Get the Bread

Best friends and business partners, KIRSTEN POE HILL and RENÉE E.
WARREN cofounded, fifteen years ago, Noelle-Elaine Media, Inc.,
a New York City–based event, management, media relations, and
video production agency with many notable corporate, non-profit,
and celebrity clients.

Ms. Warren, who is an award-winning producer, and Ms. Poe
Hill met when they were both working at CNBC, Ms. Warren in
production and Ms. Poe Hill in media relations.

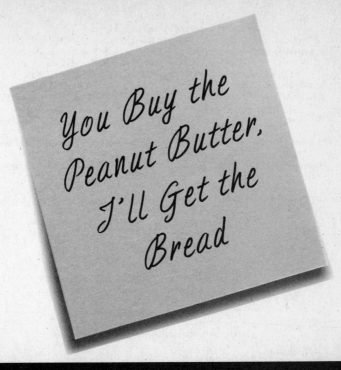

You Buy the Peanut Butter, I'll Get the Bread

The Absolutely True Adventures of Best Friends in Business

Kirsten Poe Hill & Renée E. Warren

A PLUME BOOK

PLUME
Published by the Penguin Group
Penguin Group (USA) Inc., 375 Hudson Street, New York, New York 10014, U.S.A.
Penguin Group (Canada), 90 Eglinton Avenue East, Suite 700, Toronto, Ontario, Canada
M4P 2Y3 (a division of Pearson Penguin Canada Inc.)
Penguin Books Ltd., 80 Strand, London WC2R 0RL, England
Penguin Ireland, 25 St. Stephen's Green, Dublin 2, Ireland (a division of Penguin Books Ltd.)
Penguin Group (Australia), 250 Camberwell Road, Camberwell, Victoria 3124, Australia
(a division of Pearson Australia Group Pty. Ltd.)
Penguin Books India Pvt. Ltd., 11 Community Centre, Panchsheel Park, New Delhi - 110
017, India
Penguin Group (NZ), 67 Apollo Drive, Rosedale, North Shore 0632, New Zealand (a division
of Pearson New Zealand Ltd.)
Penguin Books (South Africa) (Pty.) Ltd., 24 Sturdee Avenue, Rosebank, Johannesburg 2196,
South Africa

Penguin Books Ltd., Registered Offices: 80 Strand, London WC2R 0RL, England

First published by Plume, a member of Penguin Group (USA) Inc.

First Printing, April 2009
1   3   5   7   9   10   8   6   4   2

Ⓟ REGISTERED TRADEMARK–MARCA REGISTRADA

LIBRARY OF CONGRESS CATALOGING-IN-PUBLICATION DATA

Poe Hill, Kirsten.
  You buy the peanut butter, I'll get the bread : the absolutely true adventures of best
friends in business / Kirsten Poe Hill and Renée E. Warren.
    p. cm.
  ISBN 978-0-452-29014-3 (trade pbk.)
  1. New business enterprises—New York (State)—New York.   2. Women-owned business
enterprises—New York (State)—New York—Management.   3. Businesswomen—New York
(State)—New York—Biography.   I. Warren, Renée E.   II. Title.
  HD62.5.P5764 2009
  658.02'2—dc22

                                                                        2008046840

Printed in the United States of America

Set in Life Regular
Designed by Alissa Amell

This book is dedicated to all businesswomen and entrepreneurs who manage to do it all in spite of adversities.

Contents

Acknowledgments

From Kirsten and Renée

To our friends and family who helped us build our business by serving as volunteers during events or offering us reduced fees for their services—THANK YOU.

To our current and former clients—thank you for entrusting us with your business.

To the Windsor Management Corporation and the Kiame family, Kester Hector, Ted Reid, Rafael Martinez, Horace Flowers, Evaristo Urbaez, Richard Levychin, Sanjay Singla, Suzanne Descanvelle, Michael Mammana, Marcia Officer, Conrad Moy, Hank Mc Manus—thank you for helping us when no one else would.

To our dear friend Lisa Hew Kennedy, who gave us her old roommate Janet Hill's e-mail address and started the ball rolling. To Janet for taking the time to hear us that November and for leading us to agent Victoria Sanders. To Victoria, thank you for taking a meeting with no notice and for believing we had a story to tell. To book editor Benée Knauer—thank you for helping us tell our story and encouraging us the entire way. To Cherise Davis

Fisher—thank you for believing others will want to hear our story.

From Kirsten

First and foremost, I'd like to thank God, who shows me His love and the beauty of miracles every day. To my husband Larry, who showed me that true love is worth waiting for: we were made for each other. I cannot wait to meet the little miracle that God has given us. To my parents, Robert and Dolores, who gave me the best of themselves and showed me a world of possibilities; my sister, Deirdre, the second love of my life; her husband, Fred, who is truly my brother; and their children, Evan and Eliza, who are truly my children; to my in-laws, Lawrence and Burma, who gave me a second home and love me as their daughter—thank you all.

To my grandmother Mary Smedley—thank you making me who I am today. I did not appreciate it at the time, but your love and discipline have made me a better person. I know you are watching over me in heaven.

To my stepparents, Lucy Morales and Michael Caviano—call our family crazy, but we have all managed to work it out over the years. Thank you both for caring about our family and loving my parents.

To Leonore Pagan—my angel in heaven; you are still with me!

I have been blessed with many girlfriends—thank you all for loving me and supporting me even when I did not deserve it. You have all given me the best gift in the world—your undying friendship.

To Barbara Kelly, Tara Herman, Wayne Gilbert, Bob Martin, Neal Blake, Karen Copeland, Laura Robinson, Mark Guttman, Hilda Ayala and Brian Lewis—thanks for teaching me. To my former employees—thank you for letting me teach and learn with you.

To Max Saavedra—thank you for helping me rebuild my financial life. And even thank you to the one who helped get us into this mess—because of this experience I am stronger and sounder.

And to Renée Warren, without whom there would be no story to tell—women friends rock!

With God all things are possible—believe!!

From Renée

To my family and friends, who have made me who I am today: I would not have a story or be the person I am without your devotion to me.

To my family, which did not start with Lewis and Viola but with their parents, who laid the foundation for their governance—the love and truth of what family really is. Words cannot express the gratitude, appreciation and thanks that I have for my parents. You have given me something that money can never buy—heart.

To my late aunt Caterine, Auntie Mom, for always believing in me—I still call your name.

To my sister, Sandra, and brothers Lewis and Andrew, who have given me a sense of family, spirit and unwavering devotion no matter what the situation—and many fond memories over the years and what I hope to be many more. And to my nephews and niece,

Chadwick, Weston, Arielle, P.T. and Marshal, who during the trying times have given me the laugh I needed that only children can give.

I would need a lifetime to thank all of my friends along the way, but there are truly a few sisters without whom I could not have made it, and we often laugh that we would be buried with our secrets—so, I thank Carol Johnson Green, El'va Anderson McAfee and Lisa Warren for the long journey and keeping those secrets. And Traci Gardner Denny, Marquetta Jones, Sheilisa McNeal, Roberta Ré Kleinbard and Robin Wilson for always being there when I needed you. And, EAW for being my rock throughout the years.

Work isn't the same without friends. To all of whom I've worked with over the years, from *The Daily Press, The Virginian-Pilot*, Dow Jones, and CNBC, to the many places I've freelanced for or vendors—a simple thank-you for teaching me lessons that I carry with me today.

For thick, thin and always being by my side, Kirsten Noelle Poe Hill, my coauthor, dear friend and business partner.

Above all, GOD, who has allowed my light to shine through it all.

. . . may the Lord reward you for your kindness . . . Ruth 1:8

Introduction

To run a small business is to have a schizophrenic existence of highs and lows—of believing in yourself one minute, doubting yourself the next. Always having to put a smile on your face even as you face failure, madness and possible financial devastation—always having to push through it for the sake of the client and to prevent a mass exodus of the few employees you have.

It's all about trying to survive and, if you're lucky enough, thrive, all while maintaining a sense of dignity (when you feel desperate) and grace (when you really want to freak out). To run a business is to always have someone calling your name—the client, the employee, the intern, the solicitor, the phone company, the electric company, past due vendors, the IRS—not to mention your friends vying for any free time you have.

Everybody wants something from you yesterday.

As the requestors turn to vultures and your body and spirit into the symbolic meat they are plucking from, you fight to stay conscious, to stay aware, to believe that you are here for a purpose and for a reason.

And at the point of giving up, the sun appears—the new account is signed; the bills are paid on time; the perfect employee walks through the door; the intern who actually wants to learn can do five days a week, nine to five—and life looks good. And you know exactly why you are here: you love what you do, and—tears, fears or cheers—you are in it for the long haul.

You realize that, obstacles and difficulties aside, it was so worth it; that there is a higher joy and a sense of accomplishment in working for yourself. That through it all you have fought to control your own destiny, make your own rules and define your own sense of freedom. When you work for yourself, you are a survivor, a warrior—you have succeeded in the "road not taken" and have etched out your own independence, your own self-direction and your own wealth. Yet what you've built can't be put into just dollar amounts, but in quality-of-life amounts—the joy of working on what interests you, the joy of being able to take time for yourself and structure your business around your beliefs and attitudes. We can look back and see that we were wise enough and brave enough to capitalize on one opportunity that turned our lives around. And isn't that what life is all about? Finding what fits and who fits with you and making the most of it?

We opened Noelle-Elaine Media, a New York City–based event management, media relations and production firm, in 1993. No one could call us "green" when we opened our doors, both of us having worked in the media industry for nearly a dozen years, with companies such as CNBC, WNBC-TV, Dow Jones and Time Warner Cable. We worked as producers, journalists, publicists and sales administrators, among other industry professions, before starting our company.

Coming into it as best friends with the right experience, we were confident we would succeed—and initial success did seem to come easily. But in our fifteen years, we often found we were unprepared for the highs and the lows; for the immense emotional, physical and personal tolls it would take on us. We were equally unprepared for those herculean moments when we made something from nothing, when we got a contract against all odds or pulled off an event without a hitch, despite all forces seeming to conspire against us.

Our ability to persevere may have been evident very early on in our business. We were young, we were broke and not being able to pay rent was the least of our worries—we were having a hard time paying for lunch! We found ourselves in a dollar store and quickly started thinking of options—we had jelly in the office and realized that if we came in together on it, one could buy peanut butter and the other could buy bread and together we could make sandwiches for lunch. We quickly pooled our money and had enough sandwiches for the week; we sent the interns out for lunch, locked the doors and devoured our sandwiches in private, with none the wiser!

Looking back, making those sandwiches together said a lot about the relationship we would develop; we were instantly in tune with each other: when in crisis, we pull together; we both bring something different to the table—our personalities, the way we were raised, the way we approach work—and those differences seem to complement each other. We remain united in our effort to succeed and we realize that while we are good apart, we are amazing together. When our backs are against a wall, we automatically shift into preservation mode because we recognize the value of what we have built together—a strong friendship and a strong business. Just like peanut butter and bread go together, we go together pretty well ourselves and we have taken our similarities and our differences and made them work to our advantage. When push comes to shove, we ultimately know that two things cannot be compromised—our business and our friendship—and having that as our ongoing theme has made for a strong partnership that continues to last.

Our partnership has been like a marriage, each of us having to give and to take, to lead and to follow, to shine in the foreground and to stay in the background. We have been successful because we never stop seeking a way to make it work—and it has.

The roller-coaster ride of emotions and the struggle to succeed are what keeps our business and our friendship strong today. *You Buy the Peanut Butter, I'll Get the Bread: The Absolutely True Adventures of Best Friends in Business* is our real-life, warts-and-all tale of what you go through to make your dreams come true—and the beauty and fortune of having someone along to share the ride.

Our story is about two young friends becoming adults, and businesswomen, and facing the daily challenges of starting, growing and running a small business in the midst of maintaining and losing friendships, dating, falling in and out of love, getting married and defining who we are as women. It's part autobiographical and part business, walking you through what was going on in our lives personally and professionally and seeing how the two were intrinsically linked.

We explore our optimism in the beginning, whe[n] times shared clothes and business cards and didn't h[ave] money to eat (hence going in together on peanut butter sandwiches) and never had enough money to pay rent. And we describe the learning curves along the way—learning how to be a boss when it's your business on the line, learning how to balance partying and laughing with your employees and clients while still maintaining (you hope) their respect as boss/vendor in the morning. We take a candid look at our inner struggles to remain friends while seeing each other day in and day out—at the times when you hope you still believe in the other person and in yourself; when you rely on the other's strengths to cover your weaknesses; when you need your partner to cheer you up, because all you want to do is cry; and when you need to get the hell out of there because you're driving each other crazy. We look at the reality of small businesses and the fact that sometimes, no matter how much you outperform the big guys, some firms still won't think you're good enough—but still you dig deep and know that you are, and you keep on moving.

It all started on a snowy day in Harlem in 1993, when we were sitting in a restaurant lamenting the fact that it was cold out and we could not afford to go someplace warm for vacation. It took all of five minutes for the idea to come: we'd throw a party at that very restaurant and charge the guests! The party was a success—we made money and enjoyed ten days in Aruba and Curaçao—and ultimately that idea was the start of our business.

We had met in the fall of 1991 when we were both employees at CNBC. Renée was working as a producer, Kirsten, in media relations. Fast friends from the moment we met, our friendship was sealed the summer of '92 when we were both dealing with break-ups while at the same time planning weddings for friends and family! We had no idea that the strange juxtaposition of those experiences that summer would define and prepare us for our future in business.

Over the years, we have worked with corporations such as Ariel Mutual Funds, Ashley Stewart, *Black Enterprise* magazine, Charles Schwab, Colomer, Diageo, Disney Channel, Disney Publishing, Essence Communications, HBO, L'Oréal, *Money*, Showtime and Tribefly.com. We've also worked with several associations, foundations and nonprofit organizations. We have traveled the country and the world planning conferences and events for notables and dignitaries. We have laughed, argued, fought, hid from and run from clients and contingencies. We've had to learn cultural differences and what it means to work as women in Africa; that, with Venezuela, it's easier to get on a plane and go there, with your broken Spanish, to book an interview than to try to do it over the phone; and how having the "best legs in the Caribbean" has its business benefits. Friends and family joined us on our more interesting exploits, sometimes as employees, other times as guests, in St. Thomas, St. Martin or Palm Beach—everyone came along for the ride and shared in the fun we were having.

While working with notables and celebrities such as George W. Bush, Bill Clinton, Nelson Mandela, Hank Aaron, Muhammad Ali, Mariah Carey, Ossie Davis and Ruby Dee, Janet Jackson, LL Cool J, Samuel L. Jackson, Prince, Phylicia Rashad, Sheryl Lee Ralph, Chris Tucker, Stevie Wonder and Vanessa Williams, we quickly overcame the awe of their presence and became fierce tacticians trying to maneuver their roles during the chaos and excitement they caused around an event.

We learned how to take employees and volunteers with no experience and turn them into knowledgeable, efficient team players who could do projects in our absence. We learned to think on our feet and work with what we had. We had a never-say-die attitude that has stayed with us to this day.

Event bystanders would joke about us having roller skates on, because our team moved so fast and, no matter what, pulled off fantastic affairs with smiles on our faces. But what they did not see was the flip side—not having enough money to pay rent on your home or your business, borrowing payroll and rent money from family, having your lights and phones shut off at the office and lying to employees about the "mistake" that must have happened, realizing that your accountant was taking you to the cleaner's—all as you were trying to close on your new home. They did not see that while we were getting honors and accolades, the IRS was trying to take everything away from us and that we were slowly but surely moving toward this inevitable fate. They did not know that in our eleventh year, we almost lost it all and had to fight to survive and resuscitate our company, while keeping our employees in the dark, paying their salaries and not paying our own. It's about working through it when the bottom is falling out and believing against all odds that it will be worth it.

People have asked us over the years how we've managed to do it, how we've managed to keep the business going, work with all women and stay friends. They are amazed, yet proud that we seem to have kept it all together, along with our sense of humor and work ethic. Our public motto is "We make it happen," and that's what they saw—us running like nuts trying to make a dollar out of fifteen cents; but inside, our motto became "never let them see you sweat." *You Buy the Peanut Butter, I'll Get the Bread* unveils the real story behind our business and reveals the fallacy of several concepts: that starting a business is easy, that you can't work with your friend, that you can't rise above devastation to succeed and even grow, that you can't have it all, that you can't define your own terms for living and make it work for you. It's about recovery, acceptance, fortitude and forgiveness. It's about faith, hope and the charity of others.

It's about triggering changes, making situations work, stretching a dollar, making an impression, becoming women business owners, fostering tenacity and surviving after a crisis.

It's about the small blessings that appear in clouds of darkness. It's about two friends never giving up on a dream, and their will to succeed and remain true to themselves.

You Buy the Peanut Butter, I'll Get the Bread

Chapter 1

North and South Meet: Two Sides of the Same Coin

Kirsten

I've always said I'd never want a loaded gun in my house—my temper's too quick, my mouth too big. In a moment of anger, someone would be bound to go down and I wasn't going to let it be me. I was jumped at twelve years old—the full works, complete with crowd closing in on me and kicking. My parents dusted me off, made me return to school the next day, helped me identify the girls and take them to the authorities. They refused to allow me to do nothing, focus on fear or wallow in self-pity. I think that shaped who I am today. I promised myself that I'd never be that vulnerable again, so I learned to fight with my mouth, speak up when I see something wrong and not allow myself pity parties for too long of a time, which has had both pluses and minuses in my life.

I grew up in the Bronx, New York, and hate when people have a bad feeling about that. The northeast section of the Bronx, in the 1970s and '80s, was a pretty cool place to live. Mine was one of two black families in a predominantly Italian neighborhood (there was one Puerto Rican family, as well), and all the families had their own house and yard, and all the kids played together. What people don't know about the Bronx is that it is the soul of New York. No one sat on their asses there. Everybody got up, went to work and made sure their kids had the same work ethic. They sent their kids to school—Catholic school if they could afford it, and made sure their children knew that education was the ticket to greater things.

It was still a time when you knew the guys at the pizza parlor, and they would give you a lift home if they saw you waiting at the bus stop; you knew the dry cleaner, whose daughter was engaged to one of the older guys on our block; and you knew the shoe shop man. I grew up in a neighborhood of people just trying to hammer out a better existence. It was at the northernmost part of the city, an enclave of small three- and four-bedroom houses right near the number 2 train (last stop) and the Metro North. These were people who wanted to stay in the city, but wanted a house to live in, so every day they were willing to make the often one-hour commute into Manhattan.

We were a family of four, with Deirdre and then me. Being a same-sex second kid meant I had a perpetual chip on my shoulder, from birth. No matter what my poor parents did, I always saw myself as second, simply because I didn't get there first. So I've spent my life trying to be first at everything else.

To my parents' credit, they always let me hash it out, whether that meant a temper tantrum or tears; they let me work through it. And I rewarded them by never doing it in public! They gave me the freedom of expression and to this day I never cease to give my opinion. As a matter of fact, I don't feel honest when I can't express what I truly feel about something—not that I'm always right, I just think it would be wrong not to do so. It's something I've had to balance later in life.

My sister, Dee, is my best friend, hands down, and even though we are only fourteen months apart, she is definitely the big sister and I am definitely the baby—and I like those dynamics. Most of the women I've been attracted to as friends over the years are big sisters. I think they intrinsically understand the dynamic of dealing with the "baby"—the tantrums, the hard shell outside, soft shell inside, being considered tough when you are really so sensitive—just a basic understanding of how to "get" me. Big sisters bring a certain level of patience, empathy and understanding—and every friend I know who had a little sister had one just like me! I think it's no coincidence that Renée is a big sister. I found the right personality that matched with what I needed in a friend and business partner and I think that's why we have survived. We each have the dynamic that the other is missing.

We were a tight-knit family, and my parents stressed books over looks. Having been the first in their families to attend college, they let us know it was never a matter of *if* we wanted to go, but *where*. And every day after school our time was spent making sure we were prepared—we had extra work to do in addition to our homework. I remember Mom reading books to us, making us listen to a recording on phonics (although she would often come back into the room and find me listening to rock and roll instead) and reading over every assignment for grammar and penmanship

..ply throwing anything away that didn't meet with her approval. Looking back, I realize she was showing me how to be diligent and to never accept substandard performance in anything. To this day I like to prepare for everything. I like knowing what I have to do and setting up a plan of action. I like meeting with my team well in advance of a project's start date and putting them through the paces of fully understanding it. Nothing frustrates me more than not feeling ready or prepared—I consider it poor practice and inexcusable. I believe that as long as you have a plan in place you can adapt to any change because you have taken time to live with and understand the situation, so you know how to react—basically preparation allows you to deal with and anticipate someone else's lack of preparation.

I loved having a mom with a career. She was the oldest child and the only girl, with three brothers behind her. Her family lived in West Virginia, but she always felt destined for New York. She was always the boss and always had her own cool set of friends who did fun things like going to the ballet and theater—and she would always drag me and my sister along. We were often the only children in the group, but she realized the value of the experience she was giving us. She wasn't someone who lived in the Bronx and stayed in the Bronx; she loved Manhattan and all it had to offer her and her children. I remember seeing *The Wiz* on Broadway three times and going backstage, seeing Ben Vereen sing in *Pippin*, Rudolf Nureyev dance and Nadia Comaneci flip. Every other Wednesday Mom got paid, and that meant dinner out. We were among the first to go into the World Trade Center when it opened and we went to the Waldorf-Astoria to see Rosa Parks. Every

Christmas Mom insisted on taking us to see the windows at Macy's and Lord & Taylor and would top off the trip with ice cream at Serendipity. She was a Bergdorf Goodman- and Lord & Taylor's-shopping woman, and I loved having a smart working mom with style.

I never thought it wasn't possible to work and have a family and be successful at both. Mom was always running the show, hosting parties with her friends and dragging us along wherever she went. We were truly attached to her hip, and everyone at her job knew that when Dolores's daughters called, they had to drop everything and find her—she made it very clear that despite her important career, we were what was most important.

Dad was almost the polar opposite of my mom. A West Virginia native as well, he was the only boy with three sisters, and he and his dad were "kings of the castle" and had very traditional expectations about a woman's role, appearance and attitude. He was an *Old Yeller* and *How Green Was My Valley* type of guy, more of a solitary figure than my mom. He was a tobacco-chewing man who brought the South with him to New York. But Dad was a hard worker who never let his two jobs get in the way of his time with his girls. Dad was our weekend entertainment—the one who'd kick off Saturday with his French toast or salmon, rice and biscuits. The one who'd take us to the amusement park, the beach and the zoo and be on every roller coaster, eat every ounce of popcorn and jump in the water right with us. Yet somehow, with his traditional views, he managed to raise two extremely independent daughters. He always had a certain amount of trepidation whenever we wanted to do anything out of the ordinary (a fear that I share and have to fight in myself), but ultimately he'd give in, support and be proud of our success.

Together they raised us with love and the belief that we could do anything. They may not have always understood our choices, but even when they got divorced they made it their priority to help us make our dreams come true—in that they have always been united. Knowing that you have that kind of support is what allows you to take risks. I knew that no matter what, my family had my back—they may not agree with or understand my approach, but they are going to do everything in their power to help me succeed. That's why I never really worried about losing a job, leaving a job or starting a new business—which admittedly might have made me a little too "flip" with the tongue; I knew ultimately I had their support and could never fail.

I didn't always, however, feel so destined for success. My freshman year in high school was a giant shock. I was thirteen years old and thought I'd be fine. I chose my Catholic high school not because I was Catholic but because I'd heard that it was one of the best in the city, so I wanted to see if I could get in. I quickly saw the A's I made in elementary and junior high school drop to B's as I struggled to keep up. In my school anything below 95 was a B, anything below 85 was a C. I always felt like an idiot with my 85 average. While I can appreciate now the academic standard it set (I've always felt high school for me was harder than college or grad school), back then it made me feel inadequate. I think it threw me for a loop, and I turned inward. My sister went to a different private school and was a cheerleader, editor of her school's yearbook and honor society member, while I made a weak attempt at the track team, and did more community-based things like Project Hands. My school had 2,200 students and, at the time, less than 10 percent looked like me. Maybe that was the reason I didn't want to draw attention to myself. I just wanted to do my work and get the hell out of there. I knew I was getting a great education and I actually enjoyed a lot about school, but I just considered it a small part of my social life.

High school was made easier when I found my own niche with a group of girls who were like me. We formed our own clique and made it through together.

These were the girls who helped me survive my teenage years. We were all from the Bronx and Harlem and we were all pushed to succeed. They each taught me a lesson that I keep with me today. Staycee Benjamin taught me that it's not where you're from but where you're at. She grew up in the projects but did not let that influence her destiny in life. Tamara Nolan taught me grace, conservatism and how to be a lady: I didn't always have to be so wild and expressive—a lot of times it's simply not necessary or called for, sometimes it's important to keep your mouth shut and observe. Tamra Billinghurst—girl of all girls—taught me how to walk that line, how to be "cool" but have your own moral standards, how to be in the crowd but not "of the crowd," how to be fine with who you are and not adjust merely to fit in. Self-esteem, self-control and self-worth—these were the lessons they taught me.

Years later we would all go to college and graduate school and we would all succeed in our chosen fields. I think I had good judgment of character back then. They pulled me through high school and got me through chemistry, algebra and all of my hard subjects.

Their cool points got me invited to some of the hottest Sweet Sixteen parties and their faith in me let me know I was pretty cool myself.

In college, as in high school, I kept under the radar. My parents really wanted me to go to Syracuse since my sister was there—it meant fewer road trips for them and a discount on the tuition. I was dumb enough to go up there with a boyfriend, so I had little time for the follies of running around chasing boys, going to parties, etc. I had witnessed the wrath of my parents after my sister's freshman year and I was bound not to have it rain down on me, so I stayed with the books. I quickly hooked up with girls who were, like me, from urban areas, had gone to Catholic high school and had divorced parents and boyfriends back home. They lived on my floor and once I realized that we had all brought one-piece "footie" pajamas to college, I knew that we were all supposed to be friends.

We all managed to enjoy ourselves and, despite our boyfriends, eventually loosened up and went to parties, hung out in each other's rooms at night and studied hard. Although not an A student, I found college a lot easier than high school. The pressure was off.

Both Dee and I lived at home with Dad after college. It allowed me to work, go to school and study, without having to worry about rent. Because we lived so far north in the Bronx, grad school became easy. I had the hour and a half commute to work and the hour and a half commute after work and school to read my assignments. I felt like I never had to study because it was done by the time I got to work or home. I was an A student in grad school, I think because I had so many other things to focus on.

I enjoyed my job too. I was in the Sales and Marketing Department with Manhattan Cable (now Time Warner Cable). They had a young woman boss there who oversaw the entire department—she was under thirty; as a matter of fact, the whole department was young and fun. My job was to assist the retail sales team. That meant placing their orders when they were out, booking appointments for them, filling in for them at retail outlets when they couldn't be there and that sort of thing. Because it was Manhattan Cable, I also got to see (at least on my computer screen) where all of the celebrities lived. If you wanted cable, you had to go through us, so it was fun to find out which buildings they lived in. But my favorite thing was to go to the street fairs. New York City is known for its many summer and fall street fairs and Manhattan Cable was at all of them, recruiting customers. I would assist at the fairs and then come back and do my own analysis about booth location, the type of sales we did, how well the location worked, etc. It was a blast.

This job gave me my first taste at sales. I often had to fill in and take sales calls on the phone, follow up on leads, assist with sales reports, develop leads and even do face-to-face sales at the retail outlets. I learned what it meant to "paper" a building and the thrill of convincing a landlord to let you wire a building for cable—it mean every sale in the building was yours. I quickly had to learn not only customer service but what worked with customers—what was going to make them "sign up today," add more services or prevent them from closing an account. I learned that you had the success when you could mirror the person—listen to their needs and identify with them to make them move in the direction you wanted them to go in.

I also loved the analytical side—looking at why a certain promotion succeeded or failed and experimenting with how to make it better; how booth location, foot traffic and the selected event could affect your sales; how a sales rep who was always prepared, thorough and a natural hustler got the most sales and those who were not as prepared simply did not. I loved that as a person right out of college my thoughts mattered and that what I and other younger employees said was actually given merit. It's funny because that is one of the things our former Noelle-Elaine employees have said about us—that they felt as if they made a difference in our company, that their thoughts led to ideas that were often implemented.

But one of the most valuable lessons I learned was that men will try to hit on you at work and if you don't speak up and set your own standard, you will fail.

There was a top salesman there who always used to make uncomfortable comments to me. Things like "You look good in that dress" as he slimed by me, and made me sick. I didn't make the connection that something was really wrong—this was sexual harassment on the job before they had a name for it. I just knew that this man made me want to vomit; that he clearly thought he was free to talk to me any way he pleased and that I was not the first person he had done it to. At first I would walk in the other direction if I saw him, or try to laugh it off. I hated myself for it. I hate when a situation or a person makes me feel like I am not who I was raised to be—strong, capable, smart. His comments made me feel dirty—so why was I trying to make him feel better by brushing it off? I finally warned my boss that his comments were offensive and that he made me feel uncomfortable, so if she saw me haul off on him one day, she would know the reasons why. Again, that family support—I knew, no matter what, I would be fine, even if I had to deck someone!

Manhattan Cable had the great tradition of celebrating employee birthdays. Soon after that incident, at an office party, that salesman came near me. Loud enough for those around me to hear, I said, "You have nothing to say to me unless it is work related. Do not comment on my clothes or my hair or how I look. Do not say a word to me unless it has to do with work. Otherwise, leave me alone." And I moved away from him. I always thank Manhattan Cable because, top salesman though he was, I never had to justify my remarks and I was told they suspended him for three days for his behavior. I never had a problem with him (or anyone) after that. People told me it took chutzpah to do what I did at twenty years old, but I knew I could not live with running in fear from someone or avoiding them. I just knew that I could not let this man keep me from an invaluable learning experience. The funny thing is, I don't think he even knew what he was doing was wrong until I brought it to his attention. Other people just said, "Oh, that's just the way he is," so he assumed it was an endearing personality trait. I hope I at least made him think twice.

I must have known that I had learned a lot on the job, because within my first year there I applied for a position as supervisor. Looking back, I clearly wasn't ready on the maturity level but I felt like I knew how to do all of the work—after all, I had interned *and* worked there. Of course I didn't get the job, but at least I tried. I was also indignant enough at the time to believe that I did not get it because of my age, so I started looking for other opportunities. My former roommate Erica had received an offer from WNBC-TV after interning in production in its local programming department and suggested I try the same thing. Since I was in grad school I could still apply as a student and because I was living at home, I could afford to work five days a week, nine to five, for train fare.

People thought I was crazy for leaving a paying job to take an internship, but it was a gamble that I knew would pay off. I was accepted into the program, quit my job and interned for six months on a local program, *Positively Black*. Interning there was an education for me, as there were so many black leaders and politicians I got to meet and learn about thanks to the internship. Al Sharpton, Hazel Dukes, Harriet Michel, Wyatt Tee Walker and Calvin Butts were all on the show during my internship. Producer Bob Martin and his associate producer Neil Blake were taskmasters—they were strict on time, spelling and professionalism—but in the downtime they were also a riot. Bob and Neil would give us advice on dating and men and their candid opinions on anything we asked. At the time, the local programming department consisted of *Positively Black*, *Visiones*, *First Estate* and the specials department, all run by young professionals making their mark in the business. It was a great time to be there and a great time to learn. We got to write scripts and show promos, book guests, go on live remotes and attend in-studio tapings. It was my first experience learning about editing, taping, cameras, show development and dealing with notables. In TV it's all about timing: being late means not making air—something that could get you fired.

The local programming department also produced the *Christmas in Rockefeller Center* shows at the time, so I had the pleasure of working on that a few times. I will never forget the reaction from the women when Tony Bennett was the special guest star. From the lustful looks in their eyes, I actually thought the moms who were there to watch their daughters performing as ice skaters were going to attack him. That was always one of the best parts of working there—that along with the holiday commercials we taped. Every holiday season we would all go down to the ice skating rink and sing a holiday song that would be put on the air. You would be surprised at how many people recognized us from the commercials— people would always stop me on the street and say, "Hey, weren't you . . . ?"

As expected, the internship led to temp work, which led to a job. I was able to get a position there because Bud Carey, the general manager at the time, liked the way I answered his phone when his secretary, Barbara Lopez, was out. I always took great messages, placed the calls in priority order, sorted his mail and lined it all up on his desk. Answering his phone was part of all the interns' responsibilities, but after a while I was the only one allowed to do it. I guess he must have appreciated it because he extended my temp status until I was offered a full-time job. I always tell people that it was not the fact that I was in grad school or the fact that I had good grades that made me stand out, it was the fact that I knew how to carry myself in a professional manner and handle the phones that secured my employment there.

Karen Copeland, the local program director; Laura Robinson, her assistant; Mark Guttman, manager of Program Operations; and Hilda Ayala, manager of Sales Service, were all my bosses during my four years there. Back then, there was a strong emphasis on local programming and I got a great background in how a local TV station ran. I saw programmers come in to pitch their shows, I learned about commercial placements and where advertisers wanted to be placed, I learned about make-goods, I learned how to time shows to make sure they did not run over into valuable commercial time, I learned about the cost of buying into the Super Bowl and prepping for overtime and sudden death. Since television, radio and film management was my major in college, I can honestly say that I got to put my studies into practice. Because I worked a lot with the sales team, I also got to relive my childhood and see some of the best Broadway plays that came to town—*Les Misérables*, *Miss Saigon*, *Cat on a Hot Tin Roof*, *Grapes of Wrath*, *Cats*, you name it and I was there with my friends or family, usually in about the third row. The sales team was close-knit and generous to workers who they thought did a good job. I enjoyed working with them, and they and my managers always made sure I knew I was appreciated.

I also got to put my negotiating skills into use as I had a unique opportunity to negotiate my salary. By then Dee and I were living together. We had a large one-bedroom, one-and-a-half-bath duplex with brick walls and hardwood floors on the Upper West Side, on West End Avenue between Eighty-fourth and Eighty-fifth Streets. That part of Eighty-fourth Street was also called Edgar Allan Poe Street—we felt it was our destiny to live there since our last name was Poe. We had never lived on our own before so we were really nervous about paying our bills. We both got part-time jobs just in case we got in over our heads. I loved the neighborhood. It was only a few stops on the train from work so at the beginning I would sometimes come home on my lunch break—just to sit there and gloat.

Soon after, I was offered a promotion within one of my departments but wasn't happy with the increase that came along with it. I felt 3 percent would not justify the amount of work I was given, so I said that I regretfully had to refuse the promotion. Then, in what can only be called the chutzpah of youth, I had the idea to go talk with the director of finance for local TV, John O'Neal. He was kind enough to humor me and hear me out. As second in command at WNBC-TV, he knew me from answering the phones, as I worked in his and the general manager's private suite. I explained that I was a hard worker, working on my master's degree, that I was the only person in the department who understood this particular system they wanted me to work on and that I felt I was not being compensated enough to take on that responsibility. I told him I respected my boss, but since he, John O'Neal, controlled the money, I figured he would be the only one who could tell me if what I was asking for was crazy.

I was smart enough to realize the value of being the only one who could do a certain task and that it had to be worth something. I also knew that I had a value to the sales team—the people who brought the money in. They could rely on me to take care of their orders properly. The quicker and more efficiently I got their spots placed and ensured they weren't bumped, the quicker they got paid, so they often came directly to me to place their orders. But if worse came to worse, I think I always knew that my family would have my back. If I got fired they wouldn't let me go down like that—they would support me until I got back on my feet. They always made me feel smart and capable and that I could go out and find another job. I knew I would never be homeless or alone, so in my mind I really had nothing to lose.

Instead of firing me for going over my boss's head, O'Neal heard me out and gave me exactly what I asked for and closed with, "You never know what you're going to get unless you ask." And instead of getting mad at me, my boss was fine with it because it kept her from having to go ask for more money. I was so proud of myself. My father thought I was crazy. In his day, he never heard of anyone refusing a promotion and then asking for more money, but he was secretly proud of me.

Same with my boss—I don't think she didn't believe in me or didn't want me to get a raise. I just think she was not willing to go the extra mile since there was always a cap on budgets—and she wasn't going to be the one to rock the boat. I quickly learned I had to be my own advocate in all cases. O'Neal showed me that it was okay to be bold, especially when you are young.

After about four years there, however, I knew my time was up. Local programming was slowly but surely losing its place and I yearned to do something more creative. I knew that the longer I stayed in the most recent department, which was two and a half years, the longer I would excel at something I did not want to do. I was afraid of being trapped in a department and unable to get out, so I knew I had to make a move soon. Fortunately, I entered a program run by the Walter Kaitz Foundation, whose purpose at the time was to get minorities into management positions in the cable industry.

The guy I was dating had seen an ad for the program in *Essence* magazine and thought I might be interested. Although the organization has now pretty much changed into a Web-based recruitment site, back in the 1980s and '90s it was *the* recruitment program for minorities in cable. It was created by Walter Kaitz, a prominent leader of the California Cable Television Association. He believed that the industry needed to "build a management team reflecting an increasingly diverse U.S. population." The idea was to recruit talented and qualified minorities for various one-year training or direct-hire management and executive-level positions. This was a highly competitive program. You had to have a secondary degree in order to qualify and once you were selected as a finalist, you had to submit responses to provided case studies and project samples for the three-day selection process.

Those three days had to be the most gut-wrenching interview process I have ever experienced, but also one of the best. I have to say that everyone in that room was thoroughly interviewed and there is no question that a company would know exactly who it was hiring. For three days we met at the Hilton Hotel with anonymous cable executives (you could not know who they were so that you would not play favorites to a particular company), sharing meals and being screened by our skill sets.

The first day we were thrown into the room with a video camera and had three minutes to describe why we thought we made an excellent candidate for the program—three minutes to sell ourselves and say everything we felt they needed to know about us—all while trying to sound sincere and not horrified. Fortunately, I have never been nervous about standing up in front of a group and actually relished the assignment. I knew that if I could use my mouth I had a shot. I will never forget Sister Veronica, who taught English at my high school. She always said that whenever you are asked to present in front of an audience, always volunteer to go first—they can't compare you to anyone else and you get bonus points for having the guts to go first. So ever since then I have always been willing to present first in a public environment. I don't remember whether or not I had the option of going first, but I knew I was ready when called.

After the presentation we had dinner with the "unknown executives" who were judging us. The next day, over an eight-hour period, we went through four exercises both as team members and as individuals. We were given case studies and asked to discuss and present our solutions. The entire time the executives would sit in to hear our discussion, looking for who was taking the lead, who was developing strategy, who was creative and so on. During presentation time we would have to defend our position and explain how we came up with our answers.

Our individual assignment asked us to defend an earlier submission. Again you were brought into a room in front of a panel, but this time you were alone, defending your solutions. During the course of day two you were again eating meals and "networking" with unknown executives.

On the evening of day two you found out who wanted to interview you. I cannot remember who all the companies were who asked to meet with me, but I do know that my entire day three was booked. Ironically, the company that ended up hiring me was not a participant that day but one that reviewed my profile—it was CNBC and it was part of my current company. Even better, they wanted to hire me as a direct hire. To be honest I am sure it was a win-win situation for them. They got credit for participating in the program while at the same time got to keep their corporate numbers even by basically moving me from one department to the other. I got the benefit of learning a new and creative side of the business while getting a pay increase—so it was a good thing for me as well.

The job was as a media relations associate with the then fledgling network. The company was two years old and growing and I was excited to be a part of that growth. I had zero experience in media, but I interviewed well with my new boss, Brian Lewis—and he was young enough and crazy enough to give me a shot. I had no idea what I was walking into, but I do know that that job changed my life forever.

I got to CNBC and did not know what the heck I was doing. I literally had on-the-job training and was just trying to learn the ropes. Weeks before I started, a friend told me to look for his friend there, a woman named Renée. But all I was looking for was my esteem. I was thrown into an environment where I had absolutely no idea what I was doing and I was just trying to survive. I had no intention of looking for anyone.

About two weeks into the job I see this woman coming toward me in a conservative skirt to her knees, a ruffled shirt, big hair and an even bigger smile. I instantly knew she wasn't a New Yorker and I was instantly taken in by all of the energy surrounding her— it seemed to come into the room with her. When she opened her mouth and said, "Hi, I'm Renée. Want to go to lunch?" our fate was sealed.

That one lunch led to daily lunches as we became fast friends. Renée's optimism is what kept me at CNBC when I wanted to walk. She would check in on me and encourage me that things were going to get better. Her country ways were a needed distraction—her driving without shoes and steering the wheel with her knee while applying makeup would practically give me a heart attack! And she was always cooking, dinner and dessert—the girl actually made me wish I could at least turn on the oven—and I still say she makes the best sweet potato pie I have ever tasted. I would laugh at her attempts to be "city" and cosmopolitan and she'd just smile and ignore me—knowing that she looked good! Renée brought optimism and happiness to work and we were joined at the hip. We'd hang out after work and every weekend we spent at Central Park, Lincoln Center, Shakespeare in the Park—anything free.

Yet as different as we seemed, there were a lot of similarities. I always amused Renée with some of my sayings, which she would swear sounded just like her mother—she would always say, "Alright, Viola . . ." I think she was intrigued that a city girl had a bit of country understanding. Maybe it was because of all of the summers spent in the coal mines of Kimball, West Virginia, with my grandmother, where we had a much simpler existence—making homemade ice cream, walking "uptown" each week to pick up the mail at the post office, going to church and visiting my grandmother's friends each Sunday, going to the drive-in on the 4th of July and always being in by the 9 o'clock whistle. I am convinced that those summers in West Virginia, from the day after school let out until a day or two before school started, took the edge off of city life and shaped me into the balanced woman I became. I can appreciate rap as much as country, I know when to be aggressive, and I always begin or end with a please or thank-you. I was amazed that she had the balls of a truck driver—she is not afraid of anything or anyone, but goes about confronting it in such a way that you don't even realize you're being hit over the head! Ultimately it was if we shared the same fabric in our upbringings—family support, closeness with our siblings, expectation to succeed—just one of us in a city setting and one in a country setting. Just like I knew soon after I met my husband that we would be married, I knew Renée Warren would be my friend for life.

Renée

"Renée, finish picking those feathers off of the chickens, now!" said Mom. "I'm almost done," I replied. Dad and my oldest brother, Lewis, had just finished killing more than a half dozen chickens in the backyard. It always struck me how although their heads were chopped off, they continued to run around the yard. I would always help my mom pick the feathers off the chickens and the same question would arise: "Will we eat them?" She always explained that, no, we got our chickens from Farm Fresh, the local grocery store.

Today, she admits that she'd freeze our chickens but tell us she purchased them from the store, so that we wouldn't feel bad that we were eating the same chickens we ran around and chased in the backyard. I think I always knew, but it did make me feel better.

Whether chickens, pigs, horses, ducks or just dogs, there was always at least one and oftentimes several animals in our backyard. Though we lived in a suburban neighborhood until I was fourteen years old, my parents hailed from rural Virginia and grew up on "real" farms. So we were the only family in the neighborhood with a stable of farm animals. Our eggs came from the backyard, where my dad had planted several grapevines, apple trees and a pecan tree. As if this wasn't enough to keep us all busy, about a mile down the road we owned about four acres of land where we kept our horses, pigs and occasionally cows. There we maintained an even bigger garden—more work for me!

I really don't remember too much of my childhood in specific detail, and I attribute that to just being a happy-go-lucky kid, running around in the small town of Great Bridge in Chesapeake, Virginia. I do remember my dad would always tell us: "Whatever hand you're dealt each day, live it; no questions, just live each day." This has resonated with me as an adult. I guess it was just ingrained into us kids to work hard.

And my father did work hard, as he was the owner of a real estate construction and investing company in Norfolk, in addition to working at the U.S. Postal Service. I remember him going to work early in the morning, often leaving us surprises from the night before. We always thought these were great gifts: an Indian head nickel or some sort of candy.

As for my mom, Viola, she didn't work—I guess I should say she didn't work outside of the home, because her hands were truly full with raising four kids and all that entailed. She cooked breakfast, lunch and dinner for us every day, cleaned the house and ironed all the clothes. She did have a little help once we girls were old enough to pitch in. My sister, Sandra, and I would assist with the cooking because my dad would say, time and time again, that women must know how to cook and he didn't need a dishwasher when he had two daughters.

Sunday was always the big meal; my mom would start on Saturday preparing for her Sunday feast. That Sunday dinner always included dessert—some type of pie, cake or cookies. Everyone had their favorites, well, at least my brothers did. My sister and I were impartial and my dad would just eat everything, a good sampling of whatever delicious goodie my mom would bake. Sunday was always special—it was the start of the week, and you had to start the week off "right." My mom would wake the entire house up Sunday morning for church by yelling down the hallway: "Get up!!" Her voice was better and stronger than the intercom we had installed but never ultimately used.

Church was an integral part of our family life—I was very active and was part of the youth program and served as an usher all through my childhood. Mom had us on a schedule—before she married Dad, she was a nurse, and she used her training on us to keep us in line and "doctor us up" when necessary. She was also the local taxi, not just for us but for other kids in the neighborhood, and she often served as Dad's right hand as the office manager for his company. To this day, I don't know how she did it. She was always up before us and went to sleep after us. Her day was jam-packed—and if there was a holiday or birthday she always made us feel special with her homemade touches.

Ours was a traditional house—my brothers did the yardwork and handled the animals, and my sister and I kept the house. Everyone had their chores. While I loved cooking and baking, I also loved hanging around my dad at his office. He would call me his assistant. As I became older (college), he would let me balance his checkbooks, clean his office, answer the telephones and attend to anything else that needed to be done. Working with Dad was exciting and rewarding—it made me feel as though I made a difference.

As I said, my dad was a hard worker. He built the house I was born in and, in fact, a few of the homes in our neighborhood and a slew of other houses and apartment buildings throughout the neighboring city. After leaving the navy, Dad went to college and then to work for the post office. He worked the evening shift and by day was able to create and build his general contracting business. He started his company in 1960. While it was his passion to build and design houses, he thought it would be a great complement to his business to be able to sell homes, so later he obtained his real estate license. His company then transformed from a general contracting firm to a real estate investing firm.

My father's company provided the initial seed for the kids to get basic work experience—and that we did. We did receive a generous allowance for the work we contributed. It became a family affair. From both Mom and Dad, I developed great organizational skills, which helped me with school, work, afterschool activities and charity. Speaking of organizational skills, somewhere between taking care of and managing us kids, Mom went back to school and received a degree in business management. She, of course, took those skills to Dad's office and was able to assist him.

I coasted happily through elementary school, until sixth grade. I was diagnosed with scoliosis. Scoliosis is a condition that affects the spine, creating a curvature. The majority of scoliosis cases never progress to the point where surgery is necessary, and I was lucky they caught mine early on. Mom was told that I needed to wear a brace to control the curve progression. The brace was a full-body metal brace. At the time, they looked horrible—today they are made much better and are hardly noticeable. So, as I was about to go off to junior high school to have the time of my life (I had won a spot on the cheering squad) I was told that kind of exercise might not be best. I was crushed. I protested. I bartered with my parents and told them if they let me go without the brace during school hours, I would put the monstrosity on as soon as I got home, and keep it on.

The doctor had told my parents that I needed to wear it twenty-three hours a day and should only take it off one hour to bathe. But I was headstrong, and thought that if I did the instructed exercise given to me (double the amount) and rushed home to put the brace on and secure it in the last notch (this caused blisters), then maybe, just maybe I would not have to wear it at school. My plan worked, and my parents agreed as long as the first doctor's visit was positive. I was thrilled when at the first doctor's visit, my curve had not progressed—it maintained. However, because I was still growing, I had to continue to wear the brace.

The brace became a part of my life, a secret part of my life as none of my friends knew. Even today, many of my childhood friends do not know that I wore this *ugly* and painful metal brace. When I first got it, and would go out to the mall or to the doctor's office, people would stare at me. They saw a long steel rod that would come up the center of my body and out of my shirt in order to keep my spine straight. It was placed right under my chin and then all the way down with a plastic bucketlike contraption around my hips. Not the most attractive accessory for a junior high school student. However, whenever I got discouraged, I would think about what might have happened if I hadn't been given corrective treatment for my scoliosis and if the curve in my spine had become much worse. I might not have been able to do my favorite things such as cheerleading, jazz dance, ballet, tap or gymnastic classes.

Mom thought that I was doing too much. The more she tried to limit my participation in cheering or gymnastics, the more I would protest. I demanded that she take me to additional classes, so I could improve my dance and secure my position on the squad. I would save my allowance and even started to sell Avon so my parents would not have to pay for classes.

After the second or third visit to the doctor's, they told Mom that I was one of their best patients and the curve was not getting any worse. So, Mom and I told the doctor that I actually didn't wear the brace twenty-three hours but was taking dance and gymnastics. The doctor said this was one of the reasons why I was improving. The exercise was significant as it strengthened my back muscles. This is key for scoliosis patients. The gymnastics gave me stronger back muscles, which was great.

Even though I did not have to wear the brace at school (now), sometimes I felt like I was just hiding from the truth. While many of my classmates admired me for my abilities, my extracurricular activities and my large circle of friends, sometimes I felt shut out. I felt like I was living a lie. It was the secret that something *was* wrong with me. I often befriended those who had visible disabilities, like impaired hearing. One of my friends was deaf and I learned how to sign. I didn't like when classmates would ostracize her. They didn't think it was "cool" or maybe it was difficult to befriend her. But I thought that she and I were alike in many ways—it was just that no one knew my secret.

My parents were so supportive of me. They didn't pity me, nor did any of my siblings. It was life as usual and you just dealt with it. I think the scoliosis made me a stronger, more caring and empathic individual. But I also felt I lived in two worlds: one with a disability and one without. I think today, it is somewhat different . . . we, as a people, are more open to embracing differences. However, it was mixed emotions back then for me. I swore my siblings to silence. Growing up in the South, or at least in my house, you just didn't tell your business. And my wearing a brace was definitely a private family matter—not to be discussed.

I wasn't going to let this impairment affect what I would do in junior high or high school. I decided that I could do anything that I set my mind to—after all, I was Lewis and Viola's child and no different from anyone else. If anything, more capable. So, if you can think of a club or activity in school, I was probably a part of it. I wanted to make a difference in the student body, so I got myself elected to student government. I held every position from delegate to treasurer to citywide SCA officer. I wanted to improve my debating skills, so I tried out and made the debate team. I accepted an invitation to become a member of the Anchor Club, a group of young women who maintained a 3.0 average and who worked together in friendship and loyalty to render service to the community. I was asked to join the Honor Council—to ensure integrity within the school; I was a cheerleader from sixth grade all through high school and lettered in gymnastics. I was the head majorette and I wrote for the school paper . . . the list goes on and on. That's just in school. I still volunteered as a candy striper at the local hospital and ushered in my church. I wanted to make a difference. After all, we are here to change our society for the better.

My mom started to worry that I was doing too much and needed to curtail some of my activities, but I was *not* going to pull back, as I thought she may have thought it was too much because of "my condition."

I grew up in such a small town, one that I love to this day with all my heart. Great Bridge offers the perfect environment for raising a family. It was a small town with lots of history and values. Many of the friends I grew up with enriched my childhood. Band competitions or performing for Friday night football games was so exciting for me. Football was big in Great Bridge and the band was a large part of it. I can't remember a time when I wasn't practicing or trying to create a new routine for our majorette squad so that we could win first place.

It's ironic; many would have thought that my condition would have made me pull back or into a shell but I was actually nominated onto the Homecoming court and voted most popular in my senior class. I guess I proved what my father always said—that it's up to you! So, for me, whether or not I had scoliosis, I could still compete.

When I turned sixteen, it was truly one of the high points of my life so far, as my parents bought me a car. I had a Sweet Sixteen party with one hundred or so of my dearest friends at a local venue, and I didn't have to wear the brace.

My sister, Sandra, did my makeup, and it was just perfect. I still own the dress from that night and can fit in it! It was truly an amazing evening. The following year, it was topped, as I was a debutante for the Norfolk Medical Society. Although I could not date, because my father believed that young women should not date until eighteen or sometime after that, he allowed me to have an escort, as he had done in the past for Homecoming. My sister, the fashion maven, designed my dress. I wore long white gloves, three-inch white pumps, and a dress just for me, and of course I had a handsome escort, who I had known since sixth grade.

Although the brace belonged to me as if it were a third appendage, I felt life could not get better. I had met a whole slew of new friends as a debutante. The debutantes were chosen from around the area and we had to work together before the ball several months prior. So I had my friends from Great Bridge, but now I had more friends. I was so excited. The ball was held in Norfolk. Dad's business was there and I taught Saturday morning baton and dance classes there. The year was going well—I entered a local pageant and actually won the pageant and Miss Congeniality. I went on to state but placed first. I had double-booked myself; I had also entered, without knowing the date, Virginia's Perfect Teen Pageant, where I also placed. As my parents were very practical people, they weren't about to spend tons of money on a dress. So for the first pageant I wore my debutante dress and for the second pageant, one of my dearest friends, Tamara Gibson, lent me one of her dresses. That was it for me for the pageant circuit, as three were enough.

While in high school, I was busy, busy and didn't really think about dating seriously. Plus, Dad had this crazy rule early on about being in before dark, and even though he stretched it to eleven and then to midnight as I got older, it was hard to go out and be in before midnight. Dad always said nothing good could come to those who were out past midnight. But, after long conversations and much agony, I convinced Dad to let me stay out until midnight on prom night, and I think that I pushed it until 12:40.

I wanted to go away to school, as many of my close friends were doing. I received a scholarship to one college and I had money from one of the pageants I had entered as well—but that wasn't a choice. Dad thought it best that I attend a local school, as he did not want me to go away. All of us kids were roughly the same age. So while I was entering school, my older brother and mentor was off to law school. He had attended Old Dominion University. We were like two peas in a pod. Lewis and I were the middle children and we always did stuff together. He was leaving—he was my best friend, confidant and protector. I can remember when I was real young and would get scared, I would run to my parents' door and, unable to get in sometimes, would run to Lewis's room and he'd stay up until I fell back to sleep. Or on Saturdays when he would go to one of his sporting games, he would always bring me back a Krispy Kreme doughnut—they're still my favorite doughnut to this day (nothing compares). Whatever happened, if I missed my baton on a toss or I didn't win a pageant, or received a C on a test . . . Lewis was there. He always knew what to say . . . well, sometimes I didn't like what he said, but he was always *right* (unfortunately).

So, since Lewis was going off to school for his law degree, I wanted to do the same. My dad informed me that it was cost prohibitive, as Andrew was to enter college right behind me. And Sandra had just finished as well.

Because I protested and just knew that I would get my way, I never applied to any local schools. But my dad was not budging. He told me it didn't matter what school I attended, just as long as I studied and did well. Success was not measured by the school, but by the person and their dedication and hard work. At the very last minute, I knew that I had to go to a school, so I finally applied to Old Dominion—close to where we lived.

My fast momentum continued throughout college as I immediately joined the school paper as a reporter, ran for student government and was active on campus. While my parents paid for college, and gave me spending money and a car when I turned sixteen, I always knew it was important to provide for myself . . . a lesson our father taught us. And as the song goes: "Momma may have;

Papa may have; but God bless the child that got his own!" So, while in school, I did all kinds of jobs. I was a waitress and worked during the holidays at JCPenney. I also taught baton and dance and continued to volunteer at the local hospital. While these odd jobs proved to be rewarding, I wanted to get some real experience in what I hoped to be my chosen profession—journalism. I applied for an internship at WTKR-TV, which was the building block of my career. All of those reporter lessons from school and clubs paid off, as I was able to land the internship and later a job at WTKR, a CBS affiliate, which laid the foundation for who I am as a professional and allowed me to develop some lifelong friends. Work became my focus. I was writing, editing tape and learning the tools of the trade. After the internship was over, I didn't want it to end—luckily a tape editor position became available and the anchor, Betty Francis, suggested that I apply. I got the job as weekend tape editor. I could not believe I had a job at the number one TV station at the time. Betty was one of my mentors at the station, and one of the best reporters there. She covered the military and was always on her game. She would proof my copy and give me advice that I continue to use today. Although I was in lots of organizations, attended lots of events and knew lots of people, I was still quite sheltered (although I didn't know that at the time).

One of my major mistakes while working as a videotape editor was in a piece on the drinking age changing. I didn't drink any type of alcohol and never had an interest in it. I edited the story and highlighted people drinking beer—major error. After the eleven o'clock news, Betty called me over and asked, "Do you drink?" "No, Betty," I said. She then explained, without yelling or screaming, that beer and liquor were different. Well, I know that now, and to this day, when a young person makes an error, I return the favor that Betty taught me: explain the error, and move on.

The photographers, reporters and editors were all becoming mentors and best friends. Regina Mobley and Miriam Liggett taught me how to become a good reporter, what questions to ask, how to prepare myself before an interview—even basics like what to wear. I look at my old tapes now and laugh, as I sounded so southern. And although I live in New York City today, and think that I've lost my accent, it rears its head every now and then. The photographers would actually shoot stand-ups for me in their spare time. It truly was a family at WTKR. I toiled between the university and the station.

Working weekends, writing for the school paper, working in the student government and doing homework left little time to date. By this time, I did not have to wear the brace any longer. People would admire my posture and ask if I was a ballet dancer or model. One day in the student union building one of the fraternity brothers asked me out on a date and I said yes . . . I could not believe he had asked me out, as he was one of the most handsome guys I had seen on campus. He asked me to one of his fraternity's dances. However, there was a little problem because the dance would not be over until well after midnight, and because he was an officer with the fraternity he wanted to stay longer. I felt like a child, having to tell him that I had to be home by midnight—after all, he was an upperclassman. Sandra and I had made a deal. She would come pick me up at a nearby parking lot if he would walk me over. Needless to say, he and I didn't date too long as I had too many rules that he had to follow. Ironically, ten or so years later we bumped into one another and he told me that he had so much respect for me and my father's rules. Well, that didn't help me then. I just immersed myself back into work and school.

I double majored in criminal justice and speech communications and minored in political science. I truly enjoyed school and studying as much as work. Well, all but one class. Dr. Charles Jones was one of my first professors at ODU. I remember taking one of his tests and completely missing the mark. I had studied for the test as I always did. As a child, my parents always made us study even if we didn't have homework. Dad even built a long desk for all the kids downstairs in the second den—that desk had to be at least ten feet long. On that deadly test for an introductory political science class, I received an F. I looked at the grade on the test and could not believe it. I wanted to cry. How could that be? The teacher saw how shocked I was. After class, I informed him that something must be wrong—but it got better, as Dr. Jones curved the grades and I think my grade then became a C. Not much better, but I was determined to do well in the class. I received a B for my semester grade but I needed to prove to Dr. Jones that I was much better than a B student. Therefore, I signed up for another one of his classes and managed to earn an A. He and I were no longer adversaries. I began to have respect for him and his teaching abilities. We are friends and colleagues to this day.

The lesson I learned was that I wasn't going to be defeated. There may be things that I don't know, but with patience and dedication, I knew that I could conquer the class and receive a better grade. And in so doing, I learned a great deal.

It wasn't all work and no play, though it is hard to play when you have a curfew you're always trying to beat. One of my dearest college friends, a sorority sister and today a business associate, Marquetta (Molly) Moore, and I decided to drive to Richmond for a college fraternity party. I'm not even sure she knows this today, but I didn't tell my parents that we were going; rather, I just told them I would be staying with Molly. Molly was fortunate not to be living on campus—she had her own apartment off campus. See, I thought that if I didn't tell them then I would not be lying, as I could never lie to my parents—and that would not get me into Heaven. I was so excited because we were going to—rather, because *I* was going to—stay out late, attend this wonderful frat event, enjoy myself and even see one of my dearest and closest childhood friends, El'va Anderson, who was attending college at VCU in Richmond. El'va and I had met when we were twelve or so, during summer camp. We connected instantly and after camp would write all the time to each other. We continued to see one another every summer at camp. She too grew up in Virginia, in Nelson County, and eventually moved to New York City. Well, Molly and I figured Richmond wasn't far, and we could go and come back. I should have known that was just too plain simple. All of my friends and I believed pretty much in the same philosophies, morals and values in life, and Molly was no different. So, although Molly had her own apartment, it wasn't this wild apartment atmosphere—she was studious, kind and focused. Our wild side, if you could call it that, had us going to movies. So this adventure, for me and for us, was a stretch, but I reasoned that it would be safe—what could happen, after all, it was just a college party. Before we left her apartment, I called my parents to let them know that I was going to a fraternity party (leaving out that the party was not at ODU and about two hours away). Molly and I were considering staying overnight and leaving in the morning. But I kept thinking I should at least be back in the city, that to stay overnight would just be wrong. El'va tried to convince us to stay, as it was late, but we opted to get in my car and drive back. As fate would have it, we got a flat tire in the middle of nowhere, but probably about thirty minutes from school. We sat in the car and all sorts of things were running through our minds (this was before the advent of cell phones). What were we to do? We sat there and just stared at each other. I could only think, I lied to my parents and now it was coming back to haunt me. I swore never to omit the truth again. As we waited and I pondered my destiny, a car pulled up and luckily for us it was another college student who had attended the same party. This guy knew my brother and fixed the tire and followed us back to campus. Needless to say, we had learned our lesson.

By the time graduation came, I had worked as a weekend associate producer (I was promoted from my job as a tape editor after a year) and completed an internship at a local newspaper. On graduation day, I had full-time job offers at both the TV station and the newspaper. I had to decide on either print or broadcast media. I didn't want to make that decision right away, and wanted to take time and think about my future. I loved journalism and knew that was my destiny.

During my senior year in college, I had applied to a study abroad program in London and received the acceptance letter just after I received the job offer from the newspaper. Lewis suggested that it was a great opportunity and I had never been to London. I was quite fortunate as both employers agreed—they would put my position on hold for the summer. So off I went to analyze the British media through Southern Illinois University's International Study Abroad Program. I had saved half of the money needed and my parents gave me the other half. They weren't keen on my leaving the country, as Mom never flew—still doesn't. While we took vacations every summer, they were always within driving distance.

During the summer program our week was structured, but the weekends were ours. My new friends and I would take the train or a short flight to Paris, Brussels, Amsterdam . . . it was the right decision. No work for the summer—just learning more about my craft and playing. Upon returning home, I had to make a decision, and decided to go to the paper because I had worked two years in TV and knew that I could always come back. And the newspaper was giving me an opportunity to be a full-fledged, card-carrying reporter. I covered local government and the community. While there, I met two journalists who left an indelible mark on me: Crystal Kimpson and Candy Barr (yes, her parents did name her Candy Barr, but she is married today and can go by Candy Barr Bowen). God truly blessed me as in each adventure of my life, in each chapter, He always surrounded me with angels—people who would guide me toward pushing myself even further. I was given the job of covering the city council in Poquoson, general assignment and of course the police beat. Often interviewing people twice my age, I wanted to appear as a seasoned journalist and not a guppy reporter. As a newspaper reporter, it was key to hone your craft and move to a larger paper for success. So, after being at the *Daily Press* for about a year, I applied for a full-time internship reporting position at the *Virginia-Pilot* (this too was an entry-level position and a way to get into the larger paper). I got the job. I felt that now that I'd traveled the world and had my second job after college, it was time to move out. At twenty-one I was still living at home with my parents, in the same pink room with flower curtains and twin beds. Now there was more space, as Lewis and my sister were no longer living at home. So it was just Andrew, my parents and me in a six-bedroom home. Mom couldn't understand why I would want to move to a cramped, two-bedroom apartment I'd have to share.

Shortly after arriving at the paper, I'd met Sydney Trent, who would become my new roommate. Sydney had been at the paper for two years and was an excellent writer. She interviewed me, which I thought was interesting. "Do you smoke?" No. "I don't want lots of guests in and out of the house." I understand. The questions went on and on. . . . But I guess I passed. I broke the news to Dad and Mom (not easy), and off I went.

About two weeks prior, I'd met the man of my dreams. I was returning from a story and Regina (my mentor from the TV station) mentioned there was a reception for journalists happening that night. The TV station and the newspaper were next door to each other. I attended the event and met the most chivalrous, intelligent and handsome man. I didn't know anyone at this reception and sort of felt out of place. Everyone had a wineglass (I didn't drink at the time) in hand, and they were all seasoned professionals. This man noticed that I wasn't engaged in conversation and proceeded to engage me. A group of us stayed there until well after 11:00 p.m. (I still had that same curfew—midnight.) I tiptoed into the house and Mom was sitting on the couch waiting, just looking at me. She informed me it was 12:15. So the timing was perfect—new apartment, new rules—*mine*. Ironically, once I was on my own, I kept hearing my father's voice: "No good woman stays out past twelve." It was an internal conflict. So I managed to follow his rules even though he wasn't there. The good thing is that if there was something happening and I needed to stay out past twelve, I would not get "the look."

The gentleman I met at the reception later became my boyfriend and he was everything I thought he should be. After a year at the paper, I still didn't feel fulfilled. So Regina mentioned to me that I should attend the NABJ (National Association of Black Journalists) annual conference, as there was a career fair and nearly every media company would be there looking for candidates. I requested time off, and with résumé and résumé reel in hand, I was determined to find a job outside of Virginia. I would not return from the conference without a new job.

I had interviewed with more than twenty media outlets and had about ten follow-ups. I was focused—New York City was the number one media market and Lewis had already landed a job at Morgan Stanley as an investment banker two years prior. It was Dow Jones Newswire Service that stepped to the plate the quickest. They offered me a news associate position to start right away. I would be working for a wire service called Professional Investor Report, which covered hot stocks. I had no previous knowledge of the stock market and had a lot of work to do to catch up. I just had to break the news to my parents—because they did not think that I should be living in New York City by myself. But we managed to make a deal that if I would stay with Uncle Richard (my dad's older brother), then I could move. I would stay with my uncle for just two months or so, but it became a second home and I was there for two years. Uncle Richard was much different from Dad. He had two sons, so his rules were not as stringent, and they all made me feel right at home. I had taken the job at Dow Jones, which was a great opportunity, but less money than Virginia. I was making about $19,000 a year and in New York City it's difficult to find housing and live. Uncle Richard made it manageable. Now there was a commute because my uncle lived in Long Island. So I would get up early, early and catch the commuter train and then get on the subway to make it to work before the markets opened. The good thing was that on the train, I managed to read the *Wall Street Journal*, the *Financial Times*, the *New York Times*, and a local paper before arriving at work. On the return, I would write letters back home to my parents, my boyfriend and friends about my experiences.

On the first day of work, I remember my boss saying basically either you get it or you go back to Virginia. Well, I wasn't returning to Virginia. I needed to learn about the stock market and quickly if I were to succeed at Dow Jones. My boss suggested that I attend the New York Institute of Finance, as many of his reporters took classes there. I did, and received a certificate in finance from the school. In addition to the class I read everything I could get my hands on about Wall Street and the markets. I would often call my brother, Lewis, as he had an MBA and JD from the University of Virginia and he worked on Wall Street. I had little money left over after taxes, paying for my commute, eating out and of course shopping for new clothes. I wanted to join a club to work out but the membership fees were more than I could afford. Because I had taught dance in Virginia, I figured it couldn't be too hard to teach aerobics, but I found out that I needed to be certified, so on weekends I worked to get certified and then began teaching at a local gym on evenings and weekends. This was a great option—I could stay in shape and get paid for it.

It's good to know how to multitask. I needed to manage my main job, a part-time job and school—well, this was a lesson and skill that I learned early in life. Understanding many careers has been helpful in starting my business because on a daily basis I am multitasking. Event planning is one big juggling act.

It was destiny for me to work at Dow Jones, but just briefly. While I learned a great deal, I wasn't passionate that this was my final stop in New York City. CNBC was just developing into the financial giant it is now and was looking for journalists. At that time, there weren't lots of journalists with a strong financial background and by now, I had a year of experience and schooling under my belt. I asked around to find out who I should send my résumé to and found out that Andy Friendly was one of the senior executives at CNBC. I decided this would be my next stop. I faxed my résumé over to him and was called in for an interview. I donned my best blue suit, with news clips in hand and an attitude that this job was mine. I interviewed with several people and then they had me sit with a senior producer, Lidj Lewis, and work on his show. He and I are still friends to this day. Shows were live each hour—this was much different from working in TV in Virginia, when we were all just working on the six or eleven o'clock newscast. But I loved the hustle and bustle and felt that I was back in my element. The only position that was available at the time was overnights. I took it, working as an associate producer for *World Business*, the first show that aired on CNBC at the time. I began freelancing for many New York–based national magazines such as *Black Enterprise*, *Essence* and *Right Choices* during the day and continued to teach aerobics. It became difficult to get my sleep pattern right. I would get home around 9:00 a.m. and sleep until four-ish, interview a few people, write a story, work out and then head to work by 11:00 p.m. I had to be in at midnight. This was ironic. I was now leaving the house at midnight. Because Lewis was living in Manhattan, I would often just crash at his house instead of going back to Long Island, since he was at work during those hours and his roommate didn't mind at all. In fact, his roommate became my best friend. After about six months or so, I inquired about working on the day side. There was an opening as an associate producer on the tape desk. It involved writing, managing the editors, pulling sound bites and keeping it all together for at least six shows. I took it!

Now, this was the job that kept my heart racing. There was always a press conference from President Clinton or then Federal Reserve chairman Alan Greenspan or a senator speaking, and the producer needed the sound bite yesterday. I had to pull the right sound bite and make sure it aired. I no longer needed the workout because I was always running to make air—it was the fifty-yard dash every day. The tape playback area was a good sprint from the tape editing rooms. There was always a deadline and there was usually not enough time. This was truly a pressure-cooker environment. The producers would call demanding the sound bites now, even though we just got the tape in house five minutes prior. I had to screen the tapes, pull the sound and write what was said. Of course each show wanted something different. I was also responsible for pulling story packages for local affiliates, changing the lead and writing copy. One of my dearest friends at CNBC, Roberta Ré, used to joke that she was going to start clocking me because she swore that I would do a marathon each week if we added up the mileage.

By now, I had worked at three media outlets and this by far was my calling. It is imperative that you find your individual calling, desire and passion. We are at work longer than we are at home—if you do what you love then it never seems like work.

I loved my job and could not wait to get to work each day. I knew every senator, congressperson, mayor, cabinet member. This was essential because when pulling the sound bites, everyone needed to be properly identified. An error would not be acceptable and I could possibly lose my job. I found myself becoming a news junkie even more so. We didn't have spell-check at CNBC then, and typos were not acceptable. I was later given the responsibility to serve as one of the producers for CNBC's weekend international business show. This was my dream job and everyone I worked with I enjoyed. I was able to manage the different personalities of the reporters, producers and anchors—I knew who would always be late with a story and who would be early. This was important as I would not pair a slow reporter with a slow editor. I created a system where I would number the tapes so the various shows could avoid repeating footage that aired prior to their show. The six o'clock producer, Robert Ferraro, became like a father figure and when my car was in the shop (or stolen) he would give me a ride home, and he allowed me to leave early when I started my master's program at Columbia University.

Those angels continued to watch over me as they provided me now with my dream job and the opportunity to meet some of the most unique individuals I know. I met Carol Johnson Green (or CJ) nearly my first week at CNBC. She and I were and are inseparable and she has continued to play a major role in my life today as my confidante and sister. She was originally from South Carolina and Washington, D.C., and she had the same values, morals, energy and passion that I had.

By this time, Lewis was now getting married to Lisa, a woman I had met on my commute. It just so happened that she lived down the street from my uncle, and we had become fast friends. I had invited her to dinner with my brother and me (we often would have weekly dinners), and the rest is history.

I searched for the perfect wedding gift for Lewis and Lisa.

Something that was worthy of my brother, who I loved so much, and his new wife, who was now one of my best friends. I thought a painting would be perfect, an original. But could I afford an original piece of art? I asked my friend and editor, Alfred A. Edmond, Jr., at *Black Enterprise* magazine (I freelanced for the publication), and he told me about an amazing artist, Alonzo Adams. I called the artist and he informed me that he was having an art show. I loved his work, but there was just one problem—too expensive. The piece that I fell in love with was about $12,000—well, I can't even remember the price . . . it was just too expensive for me, it could have been $100,000—and was on hold for Maya Angelou. Well, when I found out it was on hold for her, I knew that if she could afford it, it wasn't affordable for me. The artist told me if I came to his studio I might see something else. I went to his studio and found another painting that I loved. This also was too expensive. I proceeded to beg (not the most attractive trait) him to reduce the price. My last embarrassing moment was to ask if I could pay in three or four installments because I didn't have all the money. Alonzo and I later became friends, and Kirsten and I worked with him as well. I bought the painting.

I'd broken up with my Virginia boyfriend. He wanted to have more of a commitment from me and wanted to get married, and I wasn't leaving New York City anytime soon—he was the love of my life but I wanted to follow my dreams before settling down as many of my high school and college friends had done.

He is no longer with us. He died and we never saw our future materialize.

While this was devastating, I had to continue with my life.

Time had passed.

Lewis's best friend and roommate and I had become even closer and we eventually started dating. I don't know if it had something to do with Lewis leaving and getting married, and my dear friend Carol getting married, but love was surely in the air and I had a change of heart about getting married. The bug must have hit me somewhere between pulling sound bites and hanging out in Central Park. So, when my new "love" asked me to get married after only dating for a few months, I said—*yes!*

While I had said yes, it was in theory because I am a planner, and I could not gather my thoughts to plan my wedding. I knew something was wrong, but didn't want to face it. So, on with business. Alonzo, my artist friend, mentioned to me that his roommate's girlfriend was starting a new job and that new job was at CNBC. I knew she would love CNBC as much as I did, and I told him I would welcome her with open arms. There was just one problem—the day she started I was not there. Prior to her arriving, I had left during my lunch break to pick up something from a local store but was sideswiped by a vehicle that ran a red light. The ambulance came and whisked me off to the hospital. All I could think of was, "Please call CNBC," as the four o'clock show had not been set up . . . I just remember repeating that. Eventually, it got through to them that I must have been delirious because every time they asked me how I was feeling, I would say fine, but I need to call CNBC. They made the call and one of my coworkers informed the news desk that I had been in an accident. I can say that I did discover that I had some dear friends at CNBC.

As soon as Debra Hall and Roberta Ré found out that I was at the local hospital, they had to make sure I was fine. Debra personally came to the hospital. Lisa Bryan and I had not worked together much, but she had walked pass my desk several times and later told me she wondered where I was and asked what happened. She could not believe what had happened and sent me flowers for a speedy recovery. Before long I was back to normal and at work again.

I had to put things in perspective. Before the accident, it was all about work and I didn't think that the show could go on if I wasn't at the "tape desk" pulling tape for the shows. Even today, it's hard to believe that my staff can operate without me. But I've learned that work will continue and with proper training anyone can do your job. You must always take care of yourself first!

My first day back, I was on the lookout for Kirsten, Alonzo's friend. We were on different floors, I on news and she on the business floor. I introduced myself to her and asked her to lunch—we became fast friends. I was excited to meet her—at the first meeting, I knew she was from New York, smart, witty and was about to become my best friend. It is rare that in your adult life you actually meet friends who feel like family. Kirsten soon became my family. One always needs a confidante at work. Carol had left (and moved to Egypt) and Kirsten just stepped right in. If Carol was still there, it would have been the Three Musketeers, because today, we are all the best of friends. Whereas Carol and I would run out to lunch, Kirsten and I now did that. We had so much in common. In our free time, on weekends, we would see movies, visit parks and museums. We thought we owned New York City.

What really stood out for me about Kirsten is that she was so well versed in so many subjects. She knew music, theater and most of all New York City—and that I loved.

By this time, I had finally moved out of my uncle's home and found a wonderful studio apartment on the west side of town. It was a lovely fifth-floor walk-up that my sister-in-law and Carol had helped me move into—it was a whopping 450, maybe 500 square feet, tops. My father's notion about women never living alone had to be thrown out of the window.

Friends that I grew up with could not understand why NYC or why I did not want to get married and have children. It was something I wanted, but just not now. In fact, I always fantasized about having six children—I wanted to have three and adopt three. Just, not yet.

I broke up with my fiancé (this ripped my soul, but I knew I had to do it). I decided he was not my soul mate. I felt extremely awful as he was a wonderful man. He was handsome, strong, smart—but just not for me. Feeling down, I traveled to Egypt, which helped me to come to peace with my decision. Carol had a car waiting for me and a surprise party with fifty of her closest friends. I knew no one but had a ball. While in Egypt, I visited all the sites, went shopping and met tons of new friends. By the time I returned to the States, I was able to go back to work and even face my former fiancé.

I put this behind me and moved on. When I was at Dow Jones, a colleague and I thought about starting a young hip magazine, but he didn't quite move fast enough. I was always creating something or doing something extra. In Egypt, I'd purchased tons of

Egyptian items, and upon my return I sold them at a street fair. I made enough money to buy a few new outfits and put some money in the bank. When I met Kirsten and we wanted to go on vacation, I suggested to her that we throw a party to celebrate our birthdays (our birthdays were just two weeks apart—we were destined to be friends) and charge people to attend and then we could afford a vacation without touching any of our savings.

It was perfect, she agreed, and the planning started, not just for this fantastic celebration, but for us to become business partners. Kirsten and I planning that celebration would become the impetus for our business today—we worked well together. She would start a sentence and I would finish it. She would make a suggestion and I would add her ending and the opposite would happen. How could this be—we had just barely met. The same happens today. Oftentimes, we even forget whose idea something was as we're often expanding on each other's thoughts. There was one difference: Kirsten would often say to me that it appeared something was always happening to me—from my car being stolen to being held at knifepoint to being unjustly pulled over by the police—she would say that people could tell that I was not from New York City. I'm not sure what it was, but if something bad happened, it was a lesson learned and I would not let it happen again. No one leaves this world unscathed; it's what you do with those experiences that make a difference in your life.

So, whether someone lied, cheated or stole from me, this only became my quilt for who I was. I would never let anyone else's bad behavior influence who I was, for if you let bad things stop you then there is no room for good things. And Kirsten was my new best friend—she was the "good New Yorker." People would often say to me that New Yorkers are this way or that way. But, typically, I would hear they were rude or overbearing and Kirsten wasn't any of this. Kirsten was smart, extremely witty and definitely not rude. If I had a question about life, I would often ask Kirsten, as she was my new friend, with a different perspective from all my southern friends. I loved the different perspective. Today, this enhances our business as we may approach business differently, but often will come to the same conclusion. If everyone around you shares your background, beliefs and ideologies, you never grow. Kirsten allowed me to grow as a professional and as a friend.

Chapter 2

The Start of Noelle-Elaine: Smooth Sailing

Renée

Our friendship continued to grow, from friends to "sisters" to business partners. I am one who can never sit in one place or even have one job. Throughout high school, I taught dance, worked at JCPenney, sold Avon, worked for my father, babysat and volunteered at the local hospital, and moving to New York it was no different. I taught aerobics while working at Dow Jones and freelanced as a writer for various magazines. While at CNBC, I continued to take on writing projects and when friends or work colleagues asked for my advice on how they should approach the media, I always gave it. New York is one of the most expensive places to live, and you never have enough money. Kirsten and I wanted to take a vacation—after all we deserved it. She and I shared the same birthday month (March). Kirsten suggested—rather, insisted—that we go away together.

While dining at a local eatery in Manhattan, Kirsten and I thought it would be great to celebrate our birthdays with friends and family. But, it would cost us, and after deep thought, I suggested that we host a party and charge a flat fee for those who wanted to attend our celebration. Kirsten agreed. This was the beginning of us being business partners. We hired a DJ (someone Kirsten knew) and the atmosphere was set. With the ten-dollar charge, people would have unlimited food and drinks. Don't forget, this was in 1993; the cost of living in New York has gone up significantly. But, this was still a deal. We had the entire restaurant for our friends to celebrate with us.

Well, the day of our party, it snowed—not just one inch but several. We had publicized the party so much that everyone still came out. We had a wide variety of people attending, from age twenty-one to sixty-five. Now, this was important because the mix of people proved that we could attract all audiences. In fact, an investor in the restaurant was so impressed by the caliber of people who attended he asked us if we would work for him on a few other projects. Oh, let me backtrack a little. There were nearly 250 people at this party and we made enough money to pay the restaurant bill and go on our birthday vacation to Aruba and Curaçao. Our profit had netted us enough for airfare, hotel and spending money . . . we were thrilled! If you've ever watched an *I Love Lucy* episode, then you would enjoy the many adventures Kirsten and I had. In fact, one of our colleagues at CNBC constantly called me a mix between Mary Tyler Moore and Lucy. I'm not sure if that was a compliment. Needless to say, Kirsten and I always manage to have an adventure.

After we arrived on the island of Curaçao, our second stop, we made fast friends with the locals and were invited to a party. Well, we thought that we should dress up, as they had personally invited us; so we donned our best vacation wear and when we arrived we were sorely out of place as everyone had on shorts and bikini tops. We tried to make the best of it. A few days later, we were invited to an evening party; we knew not to overdress and we both put on our "beach" attire. I put on a halter top and jean short shorts and Kirsten did the same. The problem this time was we were being invited to an office party but had no idea. I hardly need to tell you what we looked like—paid professionals. We were mortified. Our new friends assured us that we were fine! We just could not get the dress code right. This only solidified our friendship, as we were in this humiliation together.

Upon our return to the States, we marveled at how we did not have to touch our savings, 401(k) or any money from our bank accounts for our vacation. Later, the investor of the restaurant gave me a call to see if we were really serious about working for him. Kirsten and I spoke and thought to ourselves that if we were to work for him, we needed to have a company and a bank account— we needed to make ourselves legitimate. Keep in mind that oftentimes, I would write a press release for free and give free advice. This was a way we could put everything under one umbrella. We could have a media relations company and help this gentleman and build upon our professional contacts to grow our business. Kirsten agreed and our partnership was formed—just like that.

We had to think of a name and quick. Because we were both in the media and this was initially going to be a part-time job, we thought that if we used our middle names then it would not be an apparent conflict. Kirsten's middle name is Noelle and mine is Elaine. Well, there's an old rule—I thought it was a southern rule, but I'm not quite sure where I heard it—that one's middle name should start with the same letter his or her first name ends on. It gives it a nice roll off the tongue. We thought Noelle-Elaine was the perfect fit. We had a name, opened a bank account, filed papers, found an accountant and created a press kit of who we were and what services we would offer. We wanted to make sure we did not overspend, as this was a new venture. We were very cost conscious and efficient. We worked out of my apartment on the Upper West Side of Manhattan. This was a studio apartment roughly about five hundred square feet and it had what I thought was a balcony. My father, upon visiting, once laughed because he said it was illegal for me to use it as a balcony, for it was simply the rooftop. But in New York City, we all thought of outdoor space as a "hot commodity" and this was my oasis. I had placed two large trees at the end of the balcony for shade, seashells in the corner, and chairs, and on those special days I would grill outdoors and invite friends over. This space was no more than two hundred square feet, but I managed to have more than fifty people at some of my gatherings. My studio apartment served quite well as our first office and saved on costs. As a freelance writer, I already had a computer, a much-needed tool, and a local copy store on the corner, where the staff knew me and got to know Kirsten. We did all of our copying and faxing from there. And we thought the best way to save money was to have one business card with both of our names on it. Once we moved offices, we could then splurge and have two separate cards. For now, this would work.

Saving money was always at the top of our list. In fact, Kirsten would travel home each night on the crosstown bus. We only lived blocks from each other, but it was across town—from the west side where I lived to the east side for Kirsten. When it was too late, and Kirsten did not spend the night, we would gather our dollars and splurge for a taxi—that sometimes included quarters that her dad had given us. In true man fashion, he always had tons of coins.

Things were going along smoothly. In fact, as soon as we started to tell colleagues, we immediately started to build clients from those we knew. Our first client we thought was in hand, the restaurant owner—well, his venture fell through but we stayed in touch with him. It was our first lesson that you don't get everything you pursue. Fortunately for us, my financial adviser, Octavius (Ted) Reid, was doing a seminar in Hawaii and wanted media exposure. We quoted him a price for the project ($500)—we're a long way from that now—what a steal for him—and in return we would write his press release and pitch him to the Hawaiian media. This was the perfect fit for us, as Hawaii is hours ahead of New York City. So, when my show was done at 7:00 p.m., the business day was just starting in Hawaii. We could work until midnight, making as much money and getting as many hours out of each day as possible.

This first client was a huge success, as we managed to have him on several media outlets. In fact, he told us that when he returned to work he received many calls for new business.

As fate would have it, the manager/investor of the restaurant had many ventures and owned a Wall Street investment firm that was investing in a Caribbean deal and thought that we could assist him in promoting it. This was wonderful; he was going to pay us thousands of dollars to manage his media relations for his new venture. This would allow Kirsten and me to do lots of travel to the Caribbean. If my memory serves me correctly, he was paying us more than $15,000 a month for our services (this was fifteen years ago and more than we both were making individually a month—even today our monthly retainer is in the same range). We were in heaven; this was an interesting and exciting account and the traveling was the icing on the cake. What else could one ask for? We enjoyed our work—in fact, it often seemed like we weren't working at all. We were just writing and we both enjoyed writing, strategizing and speaking to the media—and we were getting paid to do this. Our business started to get more demanding as it grew, so much so that we didn't think it was fair to continue working at CNBC and working after work on our new venture, Noelle-Elaine Media. We sat down and made a few plans (developed a small business outline—nothing formal but we wrote down what we wanted to do). We wanted to gradually go full-time but wanted to make sure we were ready. We decided that we would spend our summer vacation on Martha's Vineyard with two of our best friends. Kirsten decided to ask her longtime friend Tammi, whom she had worked with at NBC, and I asked my childhood friend El'va to join us. We all pitched in and rented the house but as luck would have it my car broke down. One of my favorite cousins, Jonathan, lent us his car and we were off.

Now, his car was the ultimate show car compared to my little car at the time. Jonathan was a collector of fine things and cars were included. He owned a beautiful white Jaguar that he was kind enough to let us borrow at the very last minute. I was so nervous about driving the car, but was super careful. So, here you have Kirsten and me, plus two of our best friends, on a budget, but somehow we managed to have a beautiful four-bedroom cottage and an exquisite car for our vacation. Kirsten and I thought since we were starting a business this may be our last big vacation for who knew how long. We intended to make it memorable, and we did.

When we returned, business was good. We were hired to do several more events in the Caribbean. We had decided in April that Kirsten would leave CNBC in May—and that I would follow a month later. I didn't leave altogether, as I continued to work part-time, assisting with producing a weekend business show. It really did work out perfectly as we were part of the first set of employees at CNBC and they had promised employees who managed to stay at the company that upon their fifth anniversary their salaries would double. Well, that didn't quite play out but we did manage to receive nice bonuses, which was a good send-off. We wanted to keep this as a nest egg; we never knew when we might need it, starting that new business. We weren't planning to touch that money anytime soon. Although my small studio apartment served us well when we started our company in October 1993, as we were both going full-time we knew it was time to move. We thought it would be best to find real office space and set up our shingle officially. After scouring the streets of New York City, we found the ideal location—51 East Fourty-second Street (this was just next door to Grand Central and between Park and Madison Avenues). Who would have thought it, the girl with two ponytails from Great

Bridge with offices just off of Park Avenue? Not I! The rent was cheap, only about eighteen or twenty dollars a square foot, and it was about six or seven hundred square feet; just a bit larger than my apartment—but that was all we needed. It was a full-service building with a doorman and an elevator. My studio was a fifth-floor walk-up. It was just Kirsten and me. We thought the office was crucial because we could invite clients and have employees, which was difficult to manage in my studio apartment. We made fast friends with our cleaning lady, the maintenance men and of course the doorman. They were all instrumental in our growth as a company.

Life was good. We had an office in the heart of New York City, were managing our own accounts, were working together, had clients and were now traveling abroad. It wasn't like work at all. Why hadn't Kirsten and I done this earlier? We were spending weeks at a time in the Caribbean, hosting poolside press conferences. We would work and set up for the press conference and then the next day be in the pool. We constantly had suntans. And we were being paid for this. We stayed in the best hotels and met some of the most interesting people. Later we started to add additional clients, but the Wall Street investor was still our largest account. A dear friend of mine, someone I had met while freelance writing for a national business magazine, was launching an Africa investment fund. He called us to do the public relations, make a marketing video and plan their events. Our firm was growing and we needed some help. We really couldn't hire anyone because we still needed to receive salaries and pay the rent, electric bills and all the miscellaneous expenses, so we thought hiring interns to assist us would help get the work done. After all, at CNBC interns were crucial and both Kirsten and I had interned at television stations.

While it's easy to find college students to want to work at NBC or a local newspaper, it would be more difficult to find someone to work for a two-woman shop. As chance would have it, one of my dearest friends, Traci, would prove instrumental in one of the most pivotal times in our company. She recommended two of our best employees. Traci was from Great Bridge, and we had known each other from school, we had the same values and morals and we understood each other. She could appreciate the simple things. Living in New York with so many great Italian restaurants, it was difficult to find true New Yorkers to frequent Olive Garden—but it was my favorite and only Traci could appreciate it. Traci was like a sister—we were both majorettes in high school. She moved to New York to become an actor and had to double as a waitress. It was at this job, waiting tables, that she met Lisa Donadio and Danielle Grassi, who became future interns and employees. Both were recent graduates from Tulane University and wanted to break into media relations. A bonus for us was that they had worked in media in New Orleans. Lisa started with us as an intern. She was quick, smart and ready for the challenge. We soon started giving her more responsibility. When her roommate and best friend, Danielle, learned that Lisa was doing more than answering phones, she decided to ask us if she too could intern for us. We quickly said yes and she left her current internship and joined us. We now had a team that could push our strategies forward. We trusted them both, as my friend Traci had gotten to know them over time and she strongly recommended them as individuals with a strong work ethic, who were dependable and trustworthy. We felt like a family.

As a company, we were still loving our jobs and found each moment more interesting than the last. The Africa Fund expanded our knowledge to another continent. We were charged with informing the public about the investment opportunities in Africa. That there was more than just the horror stories that you would see on television. That investing in certain African stocks could net more than many U.S. stocks. We started pitching to the media and received great coverage from a host of publications, including the *Wall Street Journal, Fortune* and *Black Enterprise.* Even CNBC came through. The client was extremely excited about our work. With that connection, we were then hired to produce a show highlighting the investment opportunities in Africa. It allowed me to travel to Egypt and South Africa and to interview President Jerry John Rawlings of Ghana and Nelson Mandela among others. We produced the show and pulled in all of our resources. I called former anchor Karen Gibbs of CNBC, financial guru Jimmy Rogers and basically another dozen CNBC production crew members to serve as our director, editor and camera people. We managed to produce the show for one-third of what it would have cost a large production company. Michael Mammana, who had worked with me at CNBC, served as our director of photography and from that point on became our point person for all video projects. We have partnered now for more than a decade.

We won an award for producing the show, our business was growing, we were flying around the world and having what we thought was a life of fun, frills and fantastic experiences. I would not have traded it in for anything. Ironically, all of my friends from home thought that I was crazy for not wanting to settle down, get married, and have some kids. I did think about marriage, but just wasn't ready. Why stay home when I could lie on the beach, fly on private jets and ride in limos? There was no comparison: New York City or Chesapeake, Virginia—hands down Manhattan. Growing up, I loved to watch *Green Acres*. Eva Gabor starred in the show and I loved the theme song, in which the costars would argue about city versus farm life: *Green acres is the place for me. Farm livin' is the life for me. Land spreadin' out so far and wide. Keep Manhattan, just give me that countryside*—that was what my dear friend Arthene would say while I argued with her . . . that New York was my dream.

New York is where I'd rather stay. I get allergic smelling hay. I just adore a penthouse view. Darling, I love you, but give me Park Avenue.

Now, I have never lived on Park Ave., but our offices were just off of Park and have been for fifteen years. Nor was I living in a penthouse, but I just adored everything about New York City: the museums, the plays, the opportunities and the variety of people that you would meet on a daily basis. In fact, I spoke to practically everyone.

I do think that we have to live our dreams and I was doing just that. Kirsten and I had built a firm that was providing us with a lifetime of experiences. While life seemed to be moving fast and furious with excitement, there was a moment that stopped me in my tracks. My dearest friend, Arthene, died of a massive heart attack while I was traveling in Venezuela. Her husband called my mom and told me. I could not get back in time for the funeral and to this day it haunts me that I missed it. But she remains with me in my heart now and forever. Arthene's belief in living your dreams remains with me. She loved living on green acres and passed up many job offers to move to the city. She and I would have late-night calls and she would say: "Renée, you need to settle down and have kids." That wasn't my dream in my twenties. I knew I had time for marriage. I don't know if Arthene knew her future, but from the day we met at college she said that she wanted to marry her high school sweetheart, Dana, and have kids. She did just that and her dreams were met before her death. She has two beautiful kids today.

God has a different road for each of us. For Arthene, it ended earlier than one would have hoped. But she lived out her dreams as I was living my own in New York City.

After the trip from Venezuela, it was nonstop travel and Kirsten and I felt we were surely doing something right. We didn't initially have a worry about money or where money would come from. The Wall Street investor would always do things first-class. In fact, he often would even send me flowers for a job well done. We enjoyed having him as a client; eventually his business took over ours in the sense that he had so many projects that he was 80 percent of our workload. We would work for him literally all the time. In fact, too much—because if he went down, then so would we. We were aware of that at the time but he was paying us a great deal and we were reaping the benefits. Unfortunately, his business fell prey to overspending and we fell prey to his being basically our sole client. The first time his check did not arrive on time, we didn't pay any attention right away. The check was just a few days late. The next month, the check was a little later and then they just stopped coming. We had relied on him a great deal and covered all expenses—FedEx, print items, and long-distance phone bills (this was before the deregulation of the telephone companies so our telephone bills would be as high as $800 from calling the Caribbean)—his costs were ours. This was never a problem as he always paid us promptly and reimbursed all expenses.

Well, we had fallen into the mouth of wolves when he could no longer pay us. His retainer did not come; his payment of the FedEx was outstanding; his phone bill was way late. All of these items were billed directly to Noelle-Elaine Media and we were liable for them. Our name was on the line. We owed nearly $20,000 and of course we didn't have it. How would we manage to get back on our feet? The easygoing lifestyle we had came to a crashing stop.

Chapter 3

How It Changed: What Did We Do to Get Out of the Mess?

Kirsten

I clearly remember the day when, after weeks of calling, begging, praying that the client would pay us, Renée and I just looked at each other and said, "Are we going to keep asking this man for money or are we going to go out and find more money?" The honeymoon period was over. Sure, we had tanned skin, passports stamped with exotic locales and great memories, but that was about it. We had to sit there and really think about how in the heck we could run a business.

We had lulled ourselves into sleepy contentment—we enjoyed the trips, the extended vacations the business travel granted us and the international lifestyle. We had even opened an office in the _____ and hired employees, as we anticipated a full and pros- ___load. But we broke the cardinal rule that I'd learned _____ Ogilvy's *Confessions of an Advertising Man*: never have ___se retainer is most of your revenue. In the best-case scenario you were in reality no more than an employee who had to jump at their beck and call because they owned you; and in the worst-case scenario, when they went down you went down, as the revenue generated from the account that covered all of your operating costs was now gone. Unfortunately in our case it was the latter. This man had the right address, the fancy office furniture and the expensive suits—and he was going out of business. He was going down and taking us with him. It was like he dropped an anvil in our laps and we were slowly sinking.

Up until then, we were living the relatively good life. It seemed like we did not skip a beat from leaving our jobs to starting on our own business. I was living with my sister in a duplex apartment on the Upper East Side, on Eighty-ninth between Lexington and Third—three blocks from Fifth Avenue, the Guggenheim, the Met, Central Park and Jackie O.! Central Park became my own backyard—on a sunny day I'd often walk over there, strip down to my bathing suit, pull out a blanket and books and just read all day and listen to music as I watched the people walk by. Or I'd strap on my roller blades and make failed attempts to remain standing. I always loved being able to walk out of my door and do what I wanted to do without worrying about anything else, and living in Manhattan lets you have that escape.

I remember years before, taking a college friend who had never been to New York on a twelve-hour city tour where we did everything, including visiting the Guggenheim. I remember thinking, "What a nice neighborhood; I'd like to live around here one day." And there I was living in the midst of it all. I remembered *Six Degrees of Separation* being filmed right up the street; Jackie O.'s funeral and even the infamy of the Preppie Murderer, who attended a prestigious prep school one block way. That is what I loved about New York at the time—and also what I loved about my life and luck—I was always tripping into a great situation, or surviving while being around a weird one. Our parents were happy because, although they were fearful of us living on our own, they were glad we were doing it together. We had no idea about the elite reputation of the neighborhood until a woman I worked with at WNBC-TV remarked, "Oh, you live off of a named avenue—very prestigious"; apparently, living on or between Fifth, Madison, Park or Lexington meant you were living among the wealthy. But my sister's friend from New Orleans put it all into perspective when I took her on a tour of Fifth Avenue and she asked if it was where "the poor people" lived—to her, wealth meant land and houses!

I guess it goes to show that perception is everything—and to our clients and the public, the perception was that everything was fine. But the reality was quite different.

And the killer was, I saw all of the signs from this client and ignored them. That is something that also becomes a trap for a small business owner—not taking the time to interpret the signs. No one could say that Renée and I were lazy. Yes, we had the fun and the trips, but we were busting our butts working fifteen, sixteen hours a day. We just didn't make time to read the writing on the wall—we were too tired or too focused on everything except the state of our business.

This was a client who had a temper and who did not listen to his own hired counsel—not ours or those of his employees. When he was upset, he would scream and yell, which promoted, if not fear, silence. The bottom line was, he was going to do what *he* wanted to do and the rest of us had to brace ourselves and go along for the ride. It was like "The Emperor's New Clothes"— everyone saw the fool standing there naked but no one could say a word. His business was falling apart and we were watching it happen. But those checks kept coming and it gave us a false sense of security. So we didn't worry when a payment came late, then the next payment came later. We only panicked when they stopped coming at all.

Yet the whole time we thought he would recover. If nothing else, the man was scrappy—he was self-made and had come to this country and made a good living for himself. Surely he would be able to do it one more time. We prayed that he would pull more magic out of his hat as he had so many times before. And while we were on our knees, we were being knocked off of our feet—he went out of business. In the end, all we ended up with was that fancy office furniture in lieu of payment.

But we did get a few lessons as a consolation prize. From that moment forward, we would always remind clients that, in addition to paying us to "do," they paid us to "think." They paid us to use our expertise and past experience to their benefit, and while they did not have to agree with everything we said, we felt we would not be doing our due diligence if we were not allowed to give our professional opinion. We have learned that some clients have been receptive to this and others have not. Those that operate "fief-doms," whose employees can't tell them their honest opinions, are those with frustrated employees looking for a way to make a break.

nose who are open typically have employees who thrive and are allowed to grow, knowing that they have the full support of "management" behind their decisions. We spoke with our past interns for this book, and one of the things they constantly brought up was that their opinions mattered to us. They were able to bring up a suggestion in a meeting and actually see it implemented on the next project. They were able to go out and manage projects on their own and this gave them a sense of accomplishment and confidence. We think this is why so many of them have done so well after they moved on from our company.

This approach has also come in handy with the client contacts we directly reported to, as they often called upon us to be "the voice of reason" when the higher-ups would not listen to their counsel or when they were afraid to go against senior management. It's interesting that sometimes an outside source is often seen as more credible than in-house employees—that our viewpoints were often regarded with equal if not more weight than our client contacts'.

I remember one time word came down that the head of an entertainment company client wanted to hold a press conference with international dignitaries on a Friday—in the afternoon. There was absolutely no news that was being made—he just wanted to present them to the media because they were in town, even though the next day, they were meeting with the president of the United States. Apart from the fact that it was the absolute worst day and time to do a press conference, there was nothing newsworthy about the event and the media were already aware that the dignitaries were going to meet with the president; our client's employees responded with, "Well, that's what he wants to do, so we have to do it."

We literally begged them not to go forward with their plans, as it would not only embarrass their boss, but possibly ruin any diplomatic relations he was trying to establish. It was one of the moments where we had to put our foot down and demand that they stop all plans to move forward. Finally the in-house PR team asked us to write a memo with our rationale as to why this was a bad idea—and sign my name to it, not theirs. They didn't want to be the one to tell the Emperor that he had no clothes. I did, he listened and a very embarrassing situation was avoided. This man is not only wealthy, but a billionaire, and I am sure it is because he surrounds himself with good counsel—and listens to them. The interesting thing was, he never demanded a press conference. He simply had what he thought was a good idea—the problem was his staff never challenged his reasoning. Once he heard another point of view he was open to it.

This rule also gave us early indications of what type of client we were working with—if they were not open to listening, we could literally determine the level of difficulty we were going to have and usually our length of service with them.

Another cardinal rule we learned was to require at least one month's payment upon signing of the contract, and if the client fell more than a month behind in future payments, to stop work on the account. At worst, we'd only be out of one month's payment—not several.

But all of that earned wisdom wasn't doing a thing for our pockets—we still had to find new business. This client paid us five figures, while others paid us four- or sometimes three-figure fees in the hundreds. So we looked to our family and friends to start building the business back up. You never know what resources you have until you literally take inventory of everyone you know, ask them for help and ask them if they need help.

Our family and friends proved to be great resources for business. Everyone became a potential client. There was an artist who became a client—he had done a bestselling painting of me. Yes, I am forever immortalized in a painting, with an ex-boyfriend, that apparently turned out to be the artist's best seller at the time. The original was purchased by a music mogul! God bless my husband, who still allows it to hang in our home. I mean, come on, how many people can say that they have an actual painting of themselves—forget the ex—Mama is famous! Another ex-boyfriend with an internationally famous children's dance company (real men do dance ballet) worked with us; a college friend who'd opened a restaurant in Harlem years before Harlem was the place to be; a sister-in-law of Renée's who was running for local office—all of these people became our clients and helped us build up our business. And although they were not large accounts, together they helped us build our clientele and cover our costs and provided us with a variety of platforms from which to learn. Before we knew it, we were hosting art shows, restaurant openings and political fund-raisers—all things we had never done before. The breadth of experience it gave us was amazing.

I felt like we were really hustling and I loved that energy of making something happen out of nothing. I think I've always hidden my inner competitiveness, but going after business made me feel like I was fighting for survival—and we were. At CNBC I had no experience. I got a lucky break from a boss who was willing to give me a shot, but when push came to shove, I had to know my stuff. I had to learn everything—how to pitch, how to write a press release, how to deal with the media, how to deal with deadlines and show producers. I had to learn or leave and so I learned. Being at that job was the first time I had ever felt dumb. I was really out of my element and had to fight not to lose faith in myself when others around me clearly knew what they were doing. But I always said, "My parents did not raise me to embarrass myself," and I had to figure it out. This was the same situation—we had no experience, but had to survive; it was either make it work or go home, and I wasn't going home.

Other, more high-profile accounts often came from good timing and good luck. We got our first corporate entertainment account because we heard they were looking for a media relations firm of record. I called and happened to get the director of publicity on the phone. We had an immediate connection and she invited me to come in for a presentation. I know people always say that you have to have a network to make it and I heartily agree. But I always used to feel guilty about it—I hated asking people for help. I went to summer school in the ninth grade because I had refused to ask for help and tried to figure it out on my own—unsuccessfully. So for me over the years, most of my accounts have come from my gift of gab—cold calling and having a good connection with someone I've never met. While at WNBC-TV, I used to be a literacy volunteer. One senior and respected volunteer always used to tell me that I should go into sales because I had an easy way of relating to people. I later learned that he used to head a television network.

Anyway, as this particular new business meeting was out of town, I called my old college roommate, Victoria, and asked if I could stay with her. Vix is a dear friend, a woman I have known since I was seventeen, and she has always had my back. I knew we were going to be great friends in college when she, Donna DePass and I all came to college with footie pajamas. I knew she'd be a forgiving friend when we thought she'd lost the college tuition her father had sent her in cash. Only after looking through the dorm's garbage for hours with her did I realize that I had forgotten I had hidden it in her cosmetics bag for safekeeping.

I spent many a night staying at her house, often dragging her to parties, where she would sit in a corner with her boyfriend watching me dance. She knew I loved to dance and she's humored me on that since college. I was always the last person on the dance floor—even if I was dancing with myself. She stood by me when I literally danced myself sick one Thanksgiving weekend, and forced her boyfriend to clean up after me and cook for me while I lay in bed and threw up. We never agreed on boyfriends, yet she never reproached me, even when she knew that I was dating a loser; she just laughed with me at the often hysterical conclusions to these relationships. And I laughed at her when two men tried to propose to her—at her mother's funeral! I thought a fight would break out over her graveside. Needless to say, we have experienced some crazy times together.

I even lived with her and her mother for a spell when I was temping and looking for work in her city. Her mother would humor me as well—and many a night I'd come home from my temp job, sit on her bed and tell her about my day. We even started a near riot together at a movie theater when an anxious man on line began to push us to get ahead—the next thing I knew, Vix's mother, who was weak from cancer, had her cane waving in the air telling this man to get back! So Vix was family—her house was my house— and even though her boyfriends never liked me, she always stood by me and gave me a place to stay; this time was no different. Her only advice was not to leave anything out that her dog Petee could get into.

The night before the meeting, I arrived at her house, laid out the suit I was going to wear, shut the door and went to bed. The next morning I awoke to find Petee sitting on top of my suit chewing on my tube of red lipstick—which, in turn, was all over my suit! Well, the scream woke Vix up and she immediately ran to her closet to find a replacement suit that would fit me. Fortunately she had excellent taste and the suit she found looked way better than the one I was going to wear. I left for that meeting looking sharp— I mean literally, I looked so good and professional that people were stopping me on the street.

I went to the meeting and found that the rapport I had with the publicity director was even better in person and I was confident we would get the business. I just wasn't confident on how I'd get off the premises, as I did not have a car and could not find a taxi. Fortunately, one of the network's personalities saw me in my suit in the hallway and asked what I was doing there. I told him about my meeting and how I was trying to get a taxi to meet my friend. He immediately worried that I would not get a taxi out there, and although he was headed somewhere else, he got in his car and drove me to a location where I could find one, waited for it to come, and parted with, "I hope you get the job!" We got the account and the company became a client we worked with for years. But it all came about thanks to a lucky phone call, a lucky suit, a dear friend and a kind gentleman.

Renée's contacts from CNBC and her experience as a journalist came in handy and saved our butts with new business on many an occasion. People she had booked as guests on CNBC or worked with as a freelancer became clients—one of whom gave us several experiences of a lifetime. With this client we produced an award-winning documentary that allowed Renée to travel to Egypt and South Africa, where she interviewed Nelson Mandela; a private jet flew us from this same client's press conference in New York to a luncheon in D.C. on the same day and later flew us to the client's summer home in the Outer Banks, where the client rewarded us for a job well done by letting us stay there for a week. And what a job it was—as we had to organize a press conference in one city *and* a luncheon in another city that would occur only hours apart. We had to be on point and on time. We had to have an advance team in both cities as well as a stay-behind team in New York. It was a great lesson in multitasking and efficiency.

But we certainly enjoyed our rewards. I had never been on a private plane before and although I have always hated flying, I never let it keep me from traveling. I have visited Africa, Asia, Europe, South America, and the Caribbean—clutching the edge of the seat all the way over, but always knowing I'd have a life-changing experience if I made it there alive. I have jumped with the Masai tribe, gone on safari and taken a hot air balloon ride over the Serengeti in Kenya. I have visited the floating markets of Bangkok in a canoe, toured Hong Kong, survived the "Indiana Jones" adventure in Canaima Falls, hydroplaned in Margarita Island, danced in the streets in Bahia and visited the Dover Cliffs in England. I have seen the *Mona Lisa* at the Louvre and shopped on the Champs-Élysées, lain on the sands of Mauritius, partied in Spain and Portugal and tanned on beaches across the Caribbean, but I had never had my own pilot! That was truly worth the fear and the flight.

Another friend of Renée's provided an introduction that secured a ten-year account with a corporate lawyers' association that allowed us to work with general counsel from across the country. We learned to fine-tune our corporate communications skills, as this client was very different from some of the entertainment clients we had worked with. The head of the association was very detailed and specific in the way he wanted things done. From working with him we learned about timelines—a visual accounting and plan for when we were going to complete assignments, what we needed from the client to complete the assignments, and who was the responsible party. We also learned that corporate attorneys have excellent and expensive taste. While working with them we hosted events at the former Rainbow Room and planned dinner parties at Le Bernadin, among other locales; when we worked with them we got to upgrade our palates and literally tasted the finer things in life.

A fellow producer of Renée's had a husband who worked at a radio station whose boss was looking for an event management firm to host their annual dinners. Somehow I ended up taking the lead on this. Again, my rapport with their direct lead on the project, who shared the same birthday and year as me, led to a ten-year relationship that allowed us to meet and work with everyone from Muhammad Ali and Colin Powell to Mariah Carey, Stevie Wonder, LL Cool J, Diana Ross and Janet Jackson. While we may have only worked with these people for a fleeting moment in time, we learned about the entertainment media, talent management, riders, press receptions, security, stage managing a show and how star power can change the dynamics of an event. And the woman and I are still friends to this day and she danced at my wedding.

Often we were the ones booking, or assisting with booking, some of the talent and we quickly learned that a good booking would mean great coverage from the media. I will never forget the year a major recording artist was honored. At the time it was customary for all of the honorees, presenters and board members to parade through the reception on their way to the dais to generate excitement. This naturally caused guests to wait in the foyer for the arrival and always caused the program to be delayed as guests would refuse to be seated until the honorees were paraded before them.

This inevitably delayed our start time. Seeing the honorees became an anticipated occurrence, but the guests were always controlled and polite. We always hosted press receptions before the dinner to allow the media the opportunity for one-on-one interviews and photos. This was often their only chance to get time with the honorees and the system worked well because the media were happy and the client was happy as all media needs were addressed in advance and would not interfere with the dinner.

For some reason the artist was unable to attend the reception, which made the media anxious, so when she walked through, not only did the audience go crazy, but so did the media—and these were the days before crazy paparazzi coverage. They were literally charging the reception to get a shot of her—and she was gracious through it all and kept walking forward, straight into that ballroom. That was the first time I saw what the media would go through to get a shot and also understood how the public reacted to star power. Even the security team lost their minds as they were trying to pose for pictures with her (that was the last time they worked on the dinner). From working in the media, even at times on the outskirts of the media, I was never hyped about a star's presence. I was too focused on the job at hand—getting coverage, granting interviews, coordinating photo ops ("look left, center, right . . ."), etc. I was too busy "arranging talent"—telling them where to stand, where to look, what interview was next—that I rarely had time to take in who they were. It was not until this dinner that I understood how one person could incite normally well-behaved people to riot. Needless to say, the next year the client agreed to seat the guests first and bring the honorees in later—and from a private entrance.

We also learned through that client work that we had a natural rapport with the media. Having worked with the media for years before starting our business, we intrinsically knew what their needs were and how to help them get their story. I always tell people that we did not just hang up a shingle and start a business—we brought experience to the table. Years later, when we stopped working with that client and the media found out when they attended that dinner, a few called me and said, "Where in the hell were you? The dinner just isn't the same; they do not know how to work with the media and you are sorely missed." I even heard a few refused to come back because of how they were treated. Moments like that let me know that at least someone was appreciating our work and that we must have had some idea of what we were doing—even in the midst of madness.

Perhaps the single event where we really showed what we were made of was when we were hired to take over managing a dinner honoring former Negro League Baseball players. It was the first time such an event was put together. The client was already on a budget as they had fired the company previously working on the account, so they were big on goals but short on cash. As a result, we had the fun assignment of convincing baseball legends to pay for their own way to a dinner that was celebrating them—with the promise of a hotel room if they could make it. I personally remember being cursed out by at least one former player, but I completely understood where he was coming from. All I could do was promise them that once they got to New York, they would have the time of their lives. The former players were still in contact with each other and fortunately, after meeting and discussing it among themselves, they decided to risk it and come.

In addition to getting players, we handled the media, arranged the entire production, booked other baseball players and celebrities as program participants, handled all logistics with the venue and even convinced a music group that was performing elsewhere in the city to perform for us for free. We had baseballs made with the event logo, which the players signed, and miniature baseball bats engraved with the name and date of the event. The players were simply adored by the fans, who were so happy to see them, talk with them and take photos with them. After all was said and done, the players said that they had never been honored like they were that night—they could feel the love and the energy in that room. Several of them have passed on since that event—Buck O'Neil, Double Duty Radcliffe, Joe Black. We were so delighted and honored to be able to play a part in giving them such a special moment.

During that time period Renée and I learned that we were hustlers—we knew what it took to get the job done and it seemed that everything we learned from every job before this had been preparing us for running this company. People would say that it looked like we had roller skates on because they always saw us flying around getting work done. We simply did not accept the fact that something could not be accomplished. We focused on how we could make it happen, and we always did.

Chapter 4

Developing Our Business Model: What Made It Work?

Renée

Starting a company was easy, but maintaining a company proved a little more stressful. Kirsten and I needed to find the balance of our friendship and our separate work strengths. As our company grew and we did as young women, we had to find our voices and create a solid working business model that would lead us in the next phase of our business.

Kirsten and I were too foolish to realize that we had given up great jobs to start our new venture. We didn't for a moment believe that it could not work. Failure was not an option for us; working without each other was not an option. Having the proper business foundation was not in the forefront of our thoughts. Many of the people we knew thought it must be simply sublime working with one of your dearest friends and traveling the world—and this was true 99 percent of the time. However, there were some policies and a business framework we needed to put in place. While

I had sat at my father's knee for my entire life, much of his gre. business acumen did sink into my nimble and open brain. And, after all, Kirsten and I had both worked at the preeminent financial news channel, CNBC.

We knew that one of the biggest risks would be setting up business with a spouse, family member or friend. It's hard enough to be an entrepreneur, to depend on yourself for all your income. According to the U.S. Small Business Administration's June 2006 report, there were 672,800 new businesses, and 544,800 business closures. Two-thirds of new employer firms survive at least two years, and about 44 percent survive at least four. Kirsten and I were not going to be on the other side of the statistics with a closure. We would be one of the successes, no matter what it took. Nelson Mandela once said: "The greatest glory in living lies not in never falling, but in rising every time we fall." If Kirsten and I were to fall, we knew that we could brush ourselves off and make it work. We had each other.

Ours was not going to be one of the many businesses not to succeed because of working with a friend or loved one. Therefore, in our business model, we decided to always put friendship first. We treated our business like a marriage. We knew we had to compromise and we did so. We were partners—but it was business partners. Now, I believe that each and every person can choose his or her mate and whatever you decide is your choice. I preface this statement because Kirsten would constantly refer to or introduce me as her partner. This would drive me absolutely *crazy*. Coming from the South, "partner" to me meant life partner. And, while Kirsten and I were dear friends and plan to maintain our friendship and working relationship for a lifetime, I was looking for a partner of the opposite sex. So when she would introduce me as her partner, I'd turn beet red, and probably a little orange and purple. Keep in mind, Kirsten and I were together nearly every day and night, working or hanging out as girlfriends did in their twenties. Our business model initially had to start off by Kirsten introducing me as either her business partner or just friend, but "partner" never worked for me. The rest was very easy. We had created an initial plan of action early on but now we had been in business for a few years, had a few bumps and bruises and had to revisit our working model for our business. Initially, we would work side by side on all accounts.

This was not the most productive for our clients, our business or us. As the world around us changed, we had to make changes. Bill Clinton was still in office, at the end of his first term, and there was welfare reform, and the robust economy was creating the longest prosperity in U.S. history—in fact, the budget went into surplus. While America was seeing this prosperity, it was truly a good time to be in business—Kirsten and I just needed to take advantage of it. This was a time when companies needed public relations, sponsored event and video production services. We just needed to let prospective clients know who we were and what we were doing, and we were not doing ourselves any favors by being glued to one another's hips. It wasn't a time to rest on our laurels because it was a good economy. That could, and did, change. And, for a business owner, there is a different framework because you are responsible for the end results (even more so than an employee).

How do we start? we asked ourselves. One of our
ment clients constantly insisted our entire staff had to atte
meetings. Our staff at this time was small but they insisted
all managers attend. Their meetings lasted nearly four hours and
they *always* began late. Because we would arrive early, we inevitably spent nearly our entire day with them. This was the problem—if
we were meeting with them for an entire day, we could not be increasing our bottom line, and gaining new business was crucial for
the growth of our firm. Kirsten and I decided having us both attend the weekly meetings would not happen any longer. That this
would set the precedent for future clients. Only one partner would
attend meetings and even pitches. On occasion, we do both attend
a meeting but only if it's the initial setup, planning or pitch. But
this would not be a weekly event.

By separating this way, it also allowed us to have the opportunity to think and plan better for our clients and our company. With
the two of us attending a meeting, we were forced to make decisions on the spot, but when separated we were afforded the time
to ask each other's opinion without the client in front of us. And
we could toss the baton to one another; oftentimes playing good
cop-bad cop. Still to this day it is the most effective manner to
handle all business transactions. My dad would always say: "Give
me some time to sleep on it." Well, I took that to heart and now I
say and do the same thing. I believe that if you think about something overnight, you will have clarity and never (almost never)
make an unfair judgment on an issue, client or employee. You're
able to remove yourself from the situation and look at the larger
picture.

We also discovered, by not pitching business together, we could take advantage of having two senior executives as opposed to one. We could double the amount of business that we had. We were no longer a crutch for each other.

Our business model continued to develop through learning from our clients. They provided us the backdrop for many of our strategies. It was on-the-job training. Our national lawyers' account taught us that each and every client needed to have its own plan. We had always decided our goals for the clients and would write them up in paragraph form; but from these lawyer clients, who are very detailed-oriented, we learned the fundamentals of creating an extensive plan, timeline and budget. In fact, we still use the framework this client helped us develop. It has become our boilerplate for all of our media plans and we continue to get compliments on this format.

Interestingly enough, some clients may even say that it's too detailed; but for us it allows everyone to be on the same page and know who is responsible for what and at the end of the day we are not charged with something we have not committed to.

As I mentioned earlier, CNBC had provided us with the framework for a great deal of our work—especially our personal press kits and everything media related. We simply copied their format for putting together our press kit and how we wanted to be perceived. Kirsten had worked closely with the graphics person to create the design, and she and I agonized over the company color. We did not want a boring or manly blue, and pink just seemed too flighty, so we came up with a color that we thought was strong, bold and feminine—it's a cross between red and salmon.

I have always admired Michael R. Bloomberg, the financial-information mogul who currently is the mayor of my great city, New York. What I admire most is his business acumen—he created the company that bears his name and his company reflects his personality. Bloomberg, the company, provides those in the financial industry here and abroad with financial news. For me it isn't just that he had a successful business but how I thought he treated and provided for his employees. I've never worked there, but I respect the fact that while he worked there, he was a part of the team. His office was on the main floor (something that New York traders do) and the information was shared among all. As a business model, it's terrific: Bloomberg rents the terminals for thousands of dollars a month. The company is rigorously disciplined, and not just in its adherence to a seemingly old-school "hardwired" approach to providing information. Bloomberg demands absolute loyalty from all employees. With rare exceptions, people who leave are barred from being rehired. Honesty and loyalty are a fundamental basis for Kirsten and me. Habitually, when Kirsten and I are hiring someone, it's about how we feel about them. We have a small office with no more than a half dozen people working a yeoman's job and we all need to trust one another. We assume if someone comes to us for a position, they have the skills (we may need to hone them some), but we also assume they are smart. Loyalty and trust go a long way for us.

On one occasion, one of our clients (who was also a longtime friend) called to tell me that one of our employees was speaking disparagingly about us. I was devastated. This employee was someone we trusted and thought of as a "little sister"/mentee. I pulled all the employees into the conference room and, nearly in tears, I told them that we would not tolerate anyone talking negatively about the firm. If there was a problem, then we could fix it from within. But like any family, you don't take your business into the street. I discovered later that *all* the employees were petrified at this meeting. Now, I never yell, scream or raise my voice. I think people should be treated as you wish to be treated. So when I very quietly and stoically requested this meeting, one of the employees said it would have been less scary if I had screamed. Later, she said it was her worst meeting ever. Well, the person that did make the untrue remarks was eventually let go. The lesson learned for her was you never know who you are speaking to so you should never talk badly about your employer or anyone—especially when you are lying.

Back to why we love the Bloomberg model. There is this wonderful break area where employees can have lunch, dinner or snacks. All the food is free. And, if you ever have a chance to visit Bloomberg, it is the most technologically advanced, beautiful and peaceful business—especially for a media outlet, which is usually mayhem driven. There was something about Mr. Bloomberg that just struck Kirsten and me in such a way that we wanted to model some of our business practices on his. Now, we're not billionaires as he is, but we will frequently go to BJ's or Costco and purchase drinks and all sorts of goodies for our office whenever we have extra cash. Our current office space (which we have been in for ten years now) has a kitchen in it. We try to keep the refrigerator and shelves stocked with drinks and potato chips or other snacks. We think it's the small things that have encouraged our employees to stay with us for the long haul.

Our longest-termed employee, Danielle Grassi, stayed with our company for more than a dozen years. We thought of her like a sister. When she left for a life change and moved to San Diego, the entire office was saddened. We continue to speak with our sister regularly and while we can't visit her weekly, she is always in our hearts. We love e-mail. She was instrumental in developing many of our business practices without even knowing it.

To this day, we have created a basic business model and basic format for how we manage all accounts, whether it's an event or media relations or production. Initially, it was informal and not written, but now we have actually created our own guidebook. Our guidebook for the perfect interview, which we created many years ago, is so very worn that I'm sure the pages will start to crumble soon. We may need to reprint that.

As our business continued to grow, Kirsten and I continued to divide the duties of running the company, but still came together to discuss our purpose: our service offerings, strategies, infrastructure and operational processes and policies. While we didn't sit down and say, "What business model do we want to use?" much of it developed out of necessity.

In producing an event, it takes literally a village. We have volunteers around the country in all the major cities and extended arms internationally that assist us on events. We need people to work the registration desks, hostesses at the doors, direction guides, office personnel, general assistance and the list goes on. We can't hire these people on a full-time basis or even for the day as it just doesn't fit into our budget when a client pays us. But we've found that people enjoy working our events. Many find the events that we produce glamorous, exciting or simply a great learning opportunity, whether they want to enter our field or learn something new. Initially, it started with us just asking our friends and family to work the events that we were producing, but we found out that we needed more people than we knew. We started drafting flyers and submitted our requests to churches, schools and organizations. This necessity became a business model and by now we have trained thousands of volunteers who are exceptional at their craft. Some of them have gone on to work in the field, while others continue to work with us as an outlet from their regular jobs. We've known other organizations to implement our strategies or to use volunteers and wonder why their volunteers were not as effective. Well, the big difference is that we properly train our volunteers, or what we have now dubbed the NE Pit Crew. Kirsten has always espoused the seven Ps: "Proper prior planning prevents piss-poor performance." She learned this phrase from her former boss at CNBC and she took that to our company and it has become one of our mantras. We train our volunteers before each event. They never enter blindly. We hold mandatory meetings and create a volunteer guidebook. People initially think it's an easy job, but once they finish an event, they always tell us that our guidelines were critical. Depending on the event, the guidebook can be as little as five pages or as many as twenty.

Today, we have volunteers who have been with us for nearly fifteen years, working all of our events, and many of them have graduated from volunteers to team members, whom we do pay for the day or even to train the other volunteers. It's a proven business model that has worked! It is a two-way street because we always try to ensure all parties are happy at the end of the day—the client, ourselves and the volunteers. Ninety-five percent of the time we are successful.

In today's competitive landscape, it is important to be able to manage the continuous change in the marketplace. We constantly strive to create concepts that will succeed for our clients. I often equate our job to that of a gymnast. When we view a gymnast at the Olympics and she scores a 10, we think: "How easy. I could do that." However, the reality is we can't. Our jobs are very similar to that. Typically, people will see us and our staff producing an event, pacing the floor, working the registration desk or they'll see the client in the papers daily, and they'll think, we can do this ourselves. Well, we're not saying that our job is extremely difficult, we're not brain surgeons. However, I can think of occasions that clients have thought that. In fact, one client who we had worked with for a few years decided they would let us go and hire another company to do the job. Now, we often did more than we were contracted to do and would slave over every last detail. After the client had the new company in place for less than six months, they called us back because absolutely nothing was done properly. Lesson learned: it's not as easy as you think.

One of our first corporate clients was a leading business magazine, *Black Enterprise*. We started working with them on a small reception and later we were hired to represent the publisher and founder of the company as he promoted his book. We worked tirelessly on this account as we wanted to prove ourselves. Anyone who knows Earl G. Graves knows that he doesn't accept anything less than perfection. If he asked you to jump, you would ask, how high? and do it in pumps and a suit. He told us that his goal was for his book to be on the *New York Times* best-seller list. We were a part of the team to make that happen. The book was not only on that list but it was on several "best" lists. He appeared on CNBC and CNN; in *USA Today* and the *Wall Street Journal*; and on the front page nearly every major newspaper where we held a book signing. At the time, I had decided I wanted to be a vegetarian (yes, after eating pork, beef and everything else as a child). This proved almost impossible on that trip. Harriette Cole, who worked on the tour with me, was also a vegetarian and after going to more than a dozen cities we caved and had buffalo chicken wings—boy, were they good. The reason that I mention Mr. Graves is because this was truly a learning experience. While I knew media relations, I was on the road with one of the leading businessmen in the country. To this day, I believe I am a better businesswoman having worked for and with Mr. Graves. I watched his every move, phone call and interaction with other business leaders. It was better than attending business school, as I was on the road learning firsthand from this business giant. Many of the lessons that Kirsten and I took away from this experience we folded into our business model for our firm—including weekly staff meetings; putting in place corporate ideas, even though we were a smaller company; and making sure we were aware of what was going on in our company at all times (or at least most of the time).

Kirsten and I have been in all the positions and know the value of each position. We often work backwards when we create a media plan or event plan for a client. We decide what the client wants as their end result and then we figure out how to get them there.

Client Business Model

1. What are our goals? (Set goals.)
2. What value do we bring?
3. Who is our target?
4. What are our core capabilities? Do we need to bring in any outside consultants?
5. How will we get the job done?

Oftentimes we create different scenarios for the client and present them to ensure we're on the same page. This protects both of us: at the end of the project we are sure that we have met our goals. This was another business model that became law. Initially, we would speak with clients and we would all agree. But unless it's written down and you both agree, there may be conflict at the end. So, *full disclosure* is key to everyone's success. More recently, we have started having clients sign an agreement. We've noticed that people can have short memories about what they agreed to. If it is in writing then we can avoid this type of problem.

Chapter 5

Divide the Workload, Stretch the Dollar

Kirsten

We still try to be as conservative as possible with our expenses, even during the moments when the cash keeps coming in. It's a matter of common sense and a matter of survival. When you do what we do for a living, your source of revenue is always changing, sometimes from month to month, so you always have to be prepared for the downtimes. At any moment, a client can fire you, cease or reduce the scope of work on a project (which means cut your fees) or postpone a project—so you don't have much of a guarantee or protection. In addition, a lot of our clients, although long-term, are project clients, meaning they pay us over the length of the project as opposed to the length of a year. So while a certain project may bring in a great influx of cash over a few months, the reality often is there will be just as many lean months as prosperous ones. And to add insult to injury, oftentimes we have to rejustify our services every year! Clients who applaud and laud us after an event may all of a sudden have amnesia when it is time for an increase or even contract renewal. As a result, we can never take for granted that an account will be there next year and are always in a constant battle between how much to spend and how much to save.

We soon learned to pay bills according to who was more likely to shut us off sooner. With the utilities such as electricity, phone service and cable, we learned that we often had up to ninety days before any action was taken. More important things, such as health insurance, had to be paid within thirty days because God forbid someone would get sick and it had lapsed—we could not have that on our conscience!

Over the years, either by chance or desperation, we have also made changes that have saved us money. One thing we did, and still do, is use our office equipment until it literally breaks down or can't be fixed because companies don't service those models anymore. There's a saying, "Ride it till the wheels fall off"—well, that is the case with anything we buy for our office.

Most of our equipment has lasted at least ten years—a lot has lasted even longer. We had a Xerox machine that we dragged from office to office—the repairmen would call it a relic, but as long as we could get it to work, we saw no need to get rid of it. We finally acquiesced to the fact that we had to buy a new server after fourteen years when we could no longer save any documents we were working on. Our phones—though they no longer have those neat plastic covers on them that detail the extension numbers, the phone transferring doesn't work and in some cases the phones only work as speaker phones—are still in service. Even the company we purchased them from does not service them anymore, but as long as we can get it to ring and we can still dial, we will use them—and hey, we don't have to pay for a service contract anymore.

We were lucky with our first set of computers. We purchased them from a company that leased computers. Somewhere along the way the leasing company went out of business and we never had to finish payment. Still we held on to each desktop until they literally started dying one by one—but we would wait until smoke came out of the screens before we would purchase a new one. We never did massive purchases—just one at a time to save money.

Everything we have in the office could be called into service for whatever use we need. Gift baskets from clients turned into program holders for my wedding. Candles purchased for one event would come in handy for another client on a budget. It seemed like we always had a bag of tricks that we could put into service at a moment's notice if needed.

Even though we always tried to find ways to save money, we still never had an accurate accounting of where the money was going, when it was coming in, when it needed to go out, etc. Therefore things would always catch us by surprise. The lights going off would be the warning from the electric company that our bill was way past due, the phones not working would let us know that that bill was late as well. Our accountant, who we hired to oversee our bills, never seemed to know any more than we did and would only write checks when the power went out—but for a while it became our sick little way of operating. He who screamed loudest got paid; he who didn't sat on the sidelines. It seemed as if we were always robbing Peter to pay Paul. Today Renée and I always look at our budget and numbers to make sure we are on track but back then, we mistakenly left that to someone else.

The only people we made sure got paid were our employees. They were the ones helping us service our accounts. In addition, we always felt that we held their livelihoods in our hands—that they had left wherever they were working to come work with us—we could not take that for granted and leave them without a salary. No matter what, they always got paid, even when Renée and I didn't. Again, we broke the rule that says, "Always pay yourself first." But we felt we were between a rock and a hard place—we needed the employees to work on the business, we could not do it alone, so how could we not pay them?

In those moments we would at least make sure our basics were covered, like the rent on our apartments—and to be honest that was often late. Renée had one landlord that would track her down for payment—calling the office, her brother, me—anything to get paid. It didn't help that we told a white lie to help her get the apartment in the first place. A lot of people are reluctant to rent to small business owners as they fear they won't make a consistent salary (true), so when she went to see the apartment, I went with her and told them I was her boss and that this was the perfect place for her as it was walking distance from work. I also mentioned that she had no idea that I was about to give her a promotion to partner. This information made them believe she was a credible candidate. We also used that teamwork to keep another potential renter from getting the place. The other person who showed up happened to be someone I knew, so I went and pulled her away into a conversation, so Renée could work her southern charm on the landlords—and it worked. They soon learned to regret their decision, however!

I always had a better relationship with my landlords as I would beat them to the punch and call them and let them know payment would be late—they at least gave me credit for the honesty—and I never complained about the tacked-on late fees. During those years Dee and I, much to our parents' dismay, went our separate ways. She went to live in SoHo and then Brooklyn with her eventual husband, and I stayed on the Upper East Side in a studio.

I remember my conservative father's words when I told him that Dee and I were going to live apart and he protested. I said, "Well, besides, she's moving in with Fred." To which he responded, "No, she won't, because I will kill him first!"

Threats aside, I lived in that studio for six years. I had to figure out a million ways to be creative—I somehow managed to have a separate sleeping area and dining area; my fire escape was my terrace. I changed colors, changed the layout of furniture—literally every six months or so I was changing something—I did all I could do with my little box. I knew I was living in a gift from the realtor gods—a rent-stabilized apartment—and was lucky to once again be living in a great neighborhood (Eighty-third between First and Second) for a really reasonable rent.

Plus I had to save my money for takeout and laundry service; remember, I was raised by an independent mother who vowed that if she had girls she would never make them do "traditional" things such as cooking and cleaning, so I never learned. My first week in the apartment, I called my dad and said, "Hey, there's a flame coming out of the stove—does this mean I have gas or electric?"

His response was to drive over with a bucket of Kentucky Fried Chicken. He told me to eat that, and when I ran out, to go over to my sister's house so her boyfriend could feed us. It's funny how we all ended up marrying men who were excellent cooks!

But being willing to work it out in that small place kept my rent low (it increased less than $100 the entire time I was there) and allowed me (or my family) to manage the bills.

My parents would often take turns paying rent for my apartment when things were tough. I have to admit, that surprised me. My dad was always saying things like, "When are you going back to your job at NBC? Don't you miss the benefits?" But when I was in a bind, he called my mother, who always cheered me on, to figure out how they could help me survive.

That honesty in always telling landlords and family what was really happening came in handy when my sister found a charming apartment that was in a carriage house in the Clinton Hill neighborhood in Brooklyn right near where she lived. I saw the apartment and immediately fell in love—it had a skylight in the living room, large arched windows in the bedroom and bathroom that looked out onto a courtyard, a dining room, kitchen and loads of closet space; plus I would only have one neighbor in the building—a food stylist in the studio apartment next door. I had no plans to leave my beloved Upper East Side, where I had lived for ten years, and was very comfortable rearranging the furniture to make more space. But this place just spoke to me.

After my conversation with the landlord, she said, "Okay, I just need to run a credit check and I'll get back to you." I did not say anything but my heart was pounding. With so many late payments, who knew what my credit score was like? So I waited until I got home and called her. I said, "I really love the apartment and want to live there, but I am afraid that my credit score will not reflect the good person that I am. I am a small business owner and that has possibly affected my credit score. However, if you let me live there I promise I will be the best tenant you ever had and I will always try to pay my rent on time." Fortunately, Claire Wood was a business owner herself. As a matter of fact, my apartment sat right over the law firm she owned with her husband, which was on the lower level of the carriage house. She completely understood where I was coming from and agreed to rent the apartment to me.

But I had to move fast—I had a site visit scheduled in Ghana, for work, that turned out to be the same week I had to move. The landlords of my studio were happy to see me go, as they could bring the rent up to market value. I literally packed up my stuff in about two days, flew to Ghana for a week, came back, got off the plane and had my dad at my studio waiting on the moving guys and my sister in Brooklyn waiting to receive the stuff. I had to move fast and take advantage of the opportunity and I am so glad I did!

Claire was the best landlord I ever had. She understood if I was late on a payment—never more than a day or two; and she would never charge me a late fee, although I would always tack one on. In the four years that I lived there, she only increased my rent one time—by $100. She said it was more important for her to have a good tenant that she trusted. She also let me host my sister and brother-in-law's co-ed baby shower, not only in the courtyard below, which we used as the dancing area, but also in the large backyard of her house, which connected to the space. We had over seventy-five people there—on a perfect day that we still talk about. Claire and I are still in contact to this day.

In worst-case scenarios we would call on "the Bank of My Sister." Deirdre was really rocking in real estate and her commissions would always leave her enough money for short-term loans to cover our payroll. There were many times when a client's payment would come in a few days after payroll was due, so Dee would give us a temporary loan and we would always put the money back in her account. One of the reasons that she said she never worried about lending us money was because we always kept our word and paid her back when we said we would.

Although borrowing money from family and friends is a horrible business practice, it was the only way we could survive. At no point did we think about the fact that our accountant was never submitting profit-and-loss statements, that we never knew where we stood financially at any given moment and that we never knew the fiscal health of our company. We were too busy trying to exist and serve our clients—and it always managed to work out. We felt luck was on our side.

And luck was needed when it was time to move offices. We loved our space on Forty-second Street. We had gotten in at a time when the area was just being revitalized, so our rent was initially $750 a month and increases were similar to increases for rent-controlled apartments—never too much. Eventually, though, the area became hotter and our landlords less patient with our frequent late payments. When our lease was up, they decided that they were no longer in the business of small business and were seeking companies that could rent out entire floors. Needless to say, this would leave a lot of us out in the cold. There were so many small businesses in that building—the tailor who would alter our suits, the New York office of a new airline company that would let us use their fax or copier when ours was down, the human resources guy who found temps for us, the travel agent who booked tickets for us and let us pay later. We were a community of small business owners all striving to survive and we were about to be out on the street.

As luck would have it, on one of the rare days that we actually had time to venture outdoors during the workday, we ran into the exact realtor, Hank McManus, who had found us that office space. Hank immediately went to work and found us a converted apartment building on Twenty-eighth Street between Park and Lexington Avenues, which became our next office and current home. Because it was formerly an apartment, we had a bathroom with a shower and tub as well as a kitchen. We split the bedroom and made two small offices for me and Renée and then had another office built for Danielle Grassi, our vice president. Once again we were one of the first in a soon-to-be-thriving area. There are loads of restaurants and lots of shopping off of Park Avenue South, so we lucked out again with a great new space at a higher but at least affordable price.

At first we were upset that we had to leave our old office, but people immediately responded to the new space, saying that it looked more like a "PR agency" than our other space. They said our other space made us look like bankers—and it was true. We still had that office furniture from our former client, so we had all of these big wooden desks like you would see in financial companies, not creative companies. We had no idea that this new space actually helped our image as a young, trendy agency. The funny thing is, soon after we moved, 9/11 happened and we don't think the other building went ahead with the conversion.

We wanted to celebrate the first year in the new space. We got the idea to throw a Christmas party and decided that holding it in our new office was the most cost-effective way to do it. Initially, we thought that we would have about twenty people or so, which was manageable, as Renée, who also served as our office cook, could easily throw something together for a crowd that size. But as word grew and as we invited clients, friends, interns, former interns and their families, the party got bigger and bigger. But ol' Noelle-Elaine ingenuity kicked into action. My office and Danielle's office converted to coat closets. The conference room became the bar and the buffet. Danielle and Lisa, who were waitresses before they started working with us, kicked into gear as bartenders; Renée stayed home all day to cook for a crowd that was soon to become about two hundred people over the course of the evening; and I, the noncook, served as the hostess. The desks in the main area held candles and treats. Fortunately our office was long—more rectangular than square—and people easily fit into the space.

Everyone came to this party—even people we did not know. There was one woman who was drunk from another Christmas party who somehow stumbled into our party. After a few hours we realized that no one in the room knew who she was. Renée's brother Andrew and Danielle ended up having to put her in a taxi and send her home. Despite that incident, it was a great party—so good that, to this day, people ask us when we are having another one.

We always managed to find a way to make something happen. That creativity served us well when a client owed us money. They frequently had problems paying us although they would always come through. Their checks would occasionally bounce, but we eventually got paid. One time, however, they were behind two months as one check had bounced and the current month was past due, so they were in the hole for $14,000. After we called and called and called, they sent us a check—which bounced. Renée and I were poring over the bills once again trying to figure how we were going to pay them when it dawned on me that we still had that bounced check in our hands. We also had an associate at the issuing bank who kept trying to get us to move our business there. So I told Renée to call him and simply say, "We know this company is a client of your bank. We have a check from them that bounced. All we want to know is, if we redeposit the check, will the money clear?" So he monitored their account and called us when they had enough money to cover the amount owed and we immediately ran to the bank to cash the check—and it cleared. The client never called us about it—what could they say? We had been calling and calling and calling and they eventually stopped responding to us. Although they soon closed up shop, we were paid in full.

As I mentioned before, part of our problem was that we always had so many employees to pay. At one point I believe we had twelve people on the payroll—way too many for the money we were bringing in. One of the few good pieces of advice we got from our accountant at that time was to reduce our payroll—we had way more people than we could afford. We also learned the beauty of the 1099 employee, our freelancers, who we could bring in to work on projects. Once the project was over, they could leave. We didn't have to worry about their taxes, insurance, workers' compensation, etc.—all things that added to our costs. Now we always use freelancers for short-term projects. A lot of our freelancers have worked with us for years, so our clients have come to know them and are comfortable working with them. We always try to ensure that the same freelancers are assigned to the same accounts each year, as long as they are available.

And, of course, our interns—we simply would not be in business without them. Every semester we work with local schools to find them. Because we are a small company we find that our interns get more experience than they would at larger firms. They are often writing press releases, pitching media and traveling with us to various events. One intern, Tiffany Dean, actually found that she knew more than the photographer hired to work an event and had to tell him which shots to get and which notables needed to be included in a photo op. Our interns are like our employees—and the more days they can work, the more they learn. Interns, freelancers and friends have gone with us to London, Paris, Ghana, Nigeria and the Caribbean, in addition to all over the United States. They have been true and loyal to us and we owe a lot to their hard work.

And their loyalty is always put to the test. We once had an event at a hotel in the Caribbean that a client owned. The client wanted to host a Christmas party for the less fortunate children of that country. Renée and I were busy with projects in the States, so we sent my old roommate and dear friend, Erica Branch, down to tend to the event. Erica was in the media and had been a producer; she even had a few TV awards under her belt for a children's show she created and produced. At the time she was between jobs so I knew she would be the perfect candidate.

Soon after she flew down there, however, she found that the employees of the hotel had not been paid in a while and they were on the verge of a coup! She would order food and they wouldn't deliver it—they were angry and upset and were sending a message. Because they knew she worked for their "boss," they would ask her to try to find out when they were getting paid. Erica would call me collect, saying, "Help—they're not feeding me! Please find out when these people are getting paid!" Things apparently cooled off long enough for the Christmas party to take place—but things were sketchy. Apparently our publicity efforts worked because it seemed as if the entire town turned out. Eventually there wasn't enough food for the children so they had to cut cheese sandwiches in half just to feed everyone. The event turned out to be a success, but it would not have worked had Erica not toughed it out and stayed down there to make this thing happen—even at what she feared might have been the expense of her own personal safety.

This was the kind of person that, for the most part, we have always had working for us—people who believed in us and truly wanted to see us succeed. They dealt with all of the madness and craziness perhaps because in seeing us succeed, they knew they were going to succeed.

There was one intern of mine, Christina Ainsley, who I enjoyed working with, but who I had to throw out the door because I knew we could not afford to hire her and I did not want her to intern another semester but to go out and find a job. After working her final project with us I asked her where she wanted to work. Fortunately I had a contact at that company, so I told her that I would make sure she got an interview, fly her out there and pay for a hotel—all she had to do was get the job. She flew out to San Francisco, got the job and has been living there ever since—and her company loves her. My contact who got her in the door said, "Of course I knew she would be great; I know the factory that she comes from!"

By stretching the dollar by hiring interns, we were able to survive as a company—and we are able to give the real-life, practical experience that serves them wherever they go. Our freelancers are able to give us their best because they are always guaranteed a few projects a year from us so it helps their revenue stream while allowing us to save money.

We also stumbled on an idea that we still use to this day and that everyone loves. There was a time when Renée and I would give Christmas bonuses to everyone—even when we could not afford them. We would break our backs trying to come up with money that we did not have at the end of each year. One day I got a great idea. I said, "Renée, we can't afford to give them a bonus, but we are already paying them for time. Why not close down for Christmas when it is slow anyway, but pay them for the time off?" It was a simple solution—we had to pay them anyway—so why not give them time off when work was slow? Everyone loved the idea, so much so that the following year when we asked if they'd rather have the money or the time, they voted for the time. Since then we have closed down every year between Christmas and New Year's, usually equating to a week or more off—with pay, in addition to their two weeks' vacation time.

Somehow we always figured it out, always figured out a way to pay bills, and people always seemed to think that we were doing just fine—but impressions can be misleading.

Chapter 6

Making Impressions

Kirsten

Over the years we have learned that people have formed impressions about us that, no matter how hard we try, we can't change—and we have formed impressions of them.

One of the biggest misconceptions is that because we are a small company, we cannot possibly service a large account. Yet, given the chance, we have consistently outperformed larger companies. We find that large firms may take for granted that they have the business and that their reputation precedes them—we are always the "David" to their "Goliath" and always have had to prove we could do the work and manage the workload.

We actually once assisted on a book tour for Earl C. Graves, a noted African American business personality. The publishing company representing his book simply did not understand how well-known and revered the author was in the African American community. We were hired to do the book-signing events initially, but not handle the media—that was farmed out to a large agency. For each event we would ask the publisher for more books than they wanted to ship and initially they refused. And at each event they would be amazed that the bookstore would run out of books at the signing. However, Mr. Graves saw that we knew what we were doing and hired us to take over the media effort as well. Not only did we get the client in *USA Today* (cover story, no less), the *Wall Street Journal*, the *New York Times* and every major paper in the cities we traveled to, but the book was also on the *New York Times* best-seller list. We got a chance and we ran with it and have been working with him and his companies ever since.

But other people simply won't give us a chance—they can't wrap their minds around the size of our staff and our ability to service their account. We have often been "second runner-up" to large corporation pitches. There is not one time that we made a pitch for an account when I did not think we could do better than the large agency that eventually got the business.

If nothing else, after working in media for years before we started the company, Renée and I know our business, and second, we know how to pull a team together and train them to be effective and efficient when servicing an account. From handling so many events, which often come to us with short notice, we have been forced to have standard operating procedures for how we go about tackling a project. I have always said to employees, "If I drop dead, you should be able to step over me and keep going." In other words, I should not be the one holding all of the information—you should always know what to do and when to do it.

But just as clients have held mistaken impressions of us, we have held our own as well. I like accounts that tend to be less corporate and projects that are more fun. I therefore tend to bring in the accounts that are music or entertainment related, and accounts for entertainment-focused corporations. I always say it is hard to work on something that you don't enjoy. But sometimes I hold on to that belief to a fault—and that is where having a partner to balance out your logic comes in handy.

I admit to being more hotheaded than Renée. I would always say that if I got upset about something, it was just "Tuesday," but if Renée got upset, it was time to throw down. I was always quick to feel that something was not worth the aggravation. I had grand ideas about right and wrong and being taken advantage of. She was always levelheaded and in control of her emotions, a true steel magnolia. Where I was always ready to leave an account, Renée would always stress why we needed to keep the account—at least for a little while, as we had bills to pay.

But at other times, my approach worked best. There were times when we would realize that there was no longer a benefit to working with a client—not even for the money. There was one account that we had worked with for ten years where it was really time to end the relationship. They were busy people but also high-level executives who were used to people waiting for them— even if that meant waiting for hours for a meeting to start. They would reschedule the location of the meeting from one city to another, often with a moment's notice, not considering the fact that we had other clients and the travel would cost us an entire day's work. In addition, they always wanted the head of the company present. Often I would be gone all day for what would equate to an hour-long meeting.

There was no way we could continue to do business with this client—we were growing more and more frustrated with their demands and they were growing frustrated that we no longer seemed to bend to those demands. I felt like they were our parents and we were their children and we were finally getting to the point of questioning their authority and realizing that not everything they said or did was correct.

I wanted to stop immediately after their last event for the year, which was always in the fall, but Renée wanted to wait until December, as they paid us on a monthly retainer. So I agreed to bite my tongue. But the client was not blind—they knew that things had changed. We simply could not dedicate the time and commitment and, to be honest, we felt that our time was being disrespected. So when they changed a meeting at the last minute, we often would not attend, as it would conflict with other meetings we already had planned (they were used to us canceling other meetings to accommodate their changes), or we'd send an account executive in our place. So while I was waiting until December before we ended the account, they saw the writing on the wall and called me immediately after the fall event to say that they had enjoyed working with us but they needed someone who could serve them better.

It was really the best move for both of us. I never got out a "thank you for the opportunity" letter so fast in my life. I truly felt free. And although I learned so much from that client and had opportunities that I would have never had otherwise, it was time to let it go. You can never work with someone who you feel does not value you and your time—regardless of whether it is intentional or not. All I did was simmer each time a change was made and it became expected behavior that we would bend to suit their needs; we were the ones that allowed this behavior to go on for so long. Once again, I ignored my gut and we were caught off guard with the loss of revenue. Had I gone with my instinct, we would have been prepared for the loss. Fortunately it was not a big account, but with a small business, every dollar counts.

Other times my instinct to react has been right on cue. We were hired to work on a cable association dinner. The woman we worked with was simply a rude monster-diva. She was demanding, impolite and all-around unpleasant. Over the course of working with her a great employee of ours quit—and that was my final straw. I realized that we were not protecting our employees' well-being by putting them in this hostile environment. We were working with her on a mini cable conference that was to occur the next day. So that evening I called her on the phone and told her that we would show up and do the same kick-ass job that we have always done, but during the course of the evening she was not to say a word to me or anyone that I worked with. I told her that she was mean, rude and nasty and that they did not have to worry about paying us because never working with her again would be payment enough. We did the event, it went off without a hitch and she kept clear of me and my staff the whole time. The next day I wrote a full-page summary report detailing all of the positives and negatives on how they could improve the event, and also detailed my challenges with her. The president of the association asked why I had never discussed it with him, but he understood that I did not want to bother him with the details; again, we were just trying to make it happen, and we did—and we got paid. I have not seen that woman since, but she was truly the most horrible person I have ever worked with.

A few months later we got the opportunity to work on a project with the cable network where this same woman worked. As I met with the woman who would soon be our client contact, I said, "I have to be honest with you; I worked with a woman at this company who may not have the highest regard for me or my firm. I had a very unpleasant experience working with her . . . ," and I detailed what happened. Once again the candor paid off; the woman said, "Oh, don't worry about her, we all hate her too; as a matter of fact, the fact that you had challenges with her makes me want to hire you more!"—and we got the gig!

Sometimes, I swear, our saying, "We make it happen," was more trouble than it was worth. It seemed like we were always going the extra mile. It's not that clients did not appreciate us; it's that we would often take things to the next level and put more pressure on ourselves just to do a good job. As a result, we got a great reputation but often felt exhausted and unappreciated.

But those moments where we backed out or put our foot down always felt good—and even Renée would admit that sometimes it was just not worth the money. Like the time an honoree at a dinner demanded that Danielle, our vice president, personally steam her dress; or the time I backed out of working with a long-term client who actually paid well because they could never make a decision on things, always causing us to do double the work. I parted with, "I told my team they would have a good summer, and working with you will not allow that to happen." It was times like these that we had to remember that no matter how great a relationship we had with the client, this was a business—and we should never forget it.

This was really driven home when a client I had negotiated a three-year contract with, and with whom I had a great relationship, advised me after we signed the contract that I should never negotiate a three-year contract without an annual increase each year. Fortunately, I had already increased our guaranteed annual amount by way more than what we got the year before and much more than an annual increase would have allowed; but I will never forget that she told me that after the fact. She was doing her job—and she does a damn good job. She is a tough negotiator but always fair, and she always teaches me something. Yet she knew her ultimate loyalty was to the company paying her—not me—and she was 100 percent correct!

I also learned that people's impressions of me can also give me insight as to how I can improve. I think our event manager, Donna Stewart, made such a keen observation about me and Renée. I always say that Renée and I are two sides of the same coin, but Donna really brought it home when describing our management styles. She said that what she loved about me was that I provided clear direction on what I needed done—how to dot the i's and cross the t's—and took pains to make sure they were clear on their assignments and understood the project, but then I would never leave them alone to do it and I would micromanage the entire process.

What they loved about Renée was that she would make them feel as if they could do anything and throw an assignment in their lap, but provide less direction on how they should do it, or even details on the assignment. So while they were free to work as they pleased, they often needed more insight on how they were supposed to manage the project.

I thought this was amazing insight that really made me think about how I work with my team. But again, they always appreciated our willingness to listen and the fact that when push came to shove, we would all work hard, do a great job and party hard. Our favorite freelancer, former intern and former employee, Michelle Pascal, who is now a successful business owner in her own right, said that she always appreciated that after a hard event, we would all go out—boss and employees—and party hard; and to this day she knows that she can still call on us for advice as she embarks on her own projects.

No matter what, we always tried to present a professional face and worked hard. When we were broke without a cent to our name, we showed up for work every day and worked hard. When people thought we spent our lives in luxury and traveled in limos when we were really hopping on subways, we kept working hard. When the lights would go out or the employee would quit, we kept on with our work and the clients never (to our knowledge) knew the difference. I once read a quote from Denzel Washington in an interview in Oprah's magazine where he said (and I am paraphrasing here), "We do what we have to do so that we can do what we want to do." And that explains it all. You do what you have to do to stay in business, to survive, to get that next paycheck—but you stop when feel that your dignity is being compromised or you are losing more than you are gaining.

Renée

> *"Why the hell did you put this here?"*
> *"This is absolutely wrong!"*
> *"Are you crazy?"*
> *"You don't know what you're doing."*
> *"You are just incompetent!"*

Those insults were screamed at me in the middle of a black-tie event with more than one thousand people, at the front of the stage in a gorgeous ballroom, by a male executive who was about six foot two and 240 pounds. He went on for about ten minutes, screaming at the top of his lungs and with his face completely *red.*

I was mortified, embarrassed for him and me. The humiliation was nearly unbearable and the show had to start within minutes. I was a professional and needed to keep my composure. Just because he was "acting a fool" did not mean I had to do the same. While today I can write about it, it was the most embarrassing moment in my professional career, as all eyes were on this well-respected businessman who was ranting and raving about my incompetence.

First impressions are very hard to change. In fact, it takes just one fleeting look, maybe three to four seconds, for someone to evaluate you when they meet you for the first time. So, I believe it's better to make a fantastic first impression because it is simply impossible to try to change someone's mind afterward.

While some of the people in the ballroom may have known me, about eight hundred did not know who I was—they only knew this executive was calling me incompetent. We could possibly lose future business. This was not a good impression nor was it helping the start of our show. I decided not to let this executive get the best of me and since I did work for his company and not directly for him, I chose the high road and, in a quiet voice, asked him to move to the back of the stage to discuss the matter. He then whirled his arms and repeatedly said *no*. I began to be fearful for my life as I thought that he may become violent and hit me. Again, I asked him to come to the back of the stage and he did follow.

I'm not sure why he was so belligerent, rude and abusive or even why he displayed such erratic behavior; however, I did know that he was completely incorrect.

He was upset that one of the cameras was in front of his table. Well, the fact is that the camera was there and had been positioned there from the start of the day and when he should have completed a walk-through he did not notice it. This was the camera that records the show for instant playback. At this type of gala event, the large screens on the side of the stage must be recorded. If we were to move the screens, I explained to him in a very quiet voice, as there were corporate executives backstage, we could not move the cameras now as it would cause a thirty-minute delay in the start of the show.

He was not having it and wanted the cameras moved *now*. Typically, I follow directions from my clients directly, but I knew this made *no* sense and decided to pay him no attention and walked away from him. I then gathered my program participants and told them the show was about to begin. My staff had witnessed the entire episode and told me they were fearful for me. One person ran to get the client; another stood close by my side in case I needed assistance. We started the show five minutes late because of the mayhem. Well, things were running smoothly until the same gentleman ran backstage in the middle of the show with another ridiculous request. The whole night was just crazy. My point in telling this story is that impressions are everything. While I did report directly to this gentleman, all of his staff approached me that evening and said that I had handled the situation and him so gracefully. Even people in the audience approached me and the corporate sponsors backstage approached me to tell me how sorry they were that I had been put in this situation but they respected how had I handled it.

The corporate executive who screamed like a madman fired our company after this happened. I'm not sure if he remembered what he had done and was embarrassed but did not want to apologize, or if he just wanted me to go away and not be a constant reminder of his craziness. He was wrong on so many levels because moving the cameras, his initial reason for yelling, was not possible for the way the room was configured.

Whatever the reason was, I was devastated when he fired our company, as we had worked for the client for many years and felt that we were family. How could you fire your sister? We had always given 100 percent, if not more. We would work around the clock and anything they would ask, we would always produce. I sent a letter to another executive at the company to explain what had happened and he saw reason and hired us back within months. We still work with them today.

You have to be a professional at all times. A few people who approached me after the event suggested I should have put him in his place. Well, that would have just exacerbated the situation and the end result is that the impression the audience had of me was one of grace and dignity and not of a raving lunatic.

My father would always say you only have your name. I try to live by that. Now, that's not to say that I never do anything wrong, but I try to live right and to be honest, trustworthy and simply a good person by treating others as I would have them treat me. Even in the face of craziness.

It's that first impression that makes a difference. On another occasion, our team was doing a large-scale event with celebrities, dignitaries and key notables. As the stage producer, of course I'm always onstage or backstage. At this particular event, the president of the organization was onstage giving her keynote speech when the city mayor's advance man came backstage and said that the mayor wanted to go on "right now." That was next to impossible as we were in the middle of a program. So I politely told him no, but that I could place the mayor in the program right after the dinner break. He was not having it. He went back and chatted with the mayor only to come back to the stage to say the mayor *must* speak now. I said, "No, but we can make it happen after the program." My allegiance was to my client—my concern was that she not be interrupted, and this would clearly disrupt the program. The advance man came to the stage about four times, making noise and ranting about how his boss had to go on. I kept my composure and said that it was not possible, and repeated that I could make a smooth transition after the dinner break. He eventually just left because I could not accommodate his wishes at that present time. After the show was over, I told the client what had happened and she was fine with it. However, later that evening the advance man told a different story. He told the president of the company and his right-hand person that I was yelling and was very disrespectful to the mayor.

The client knew this was not my character and did not believe the advance man.

Lesson—not only a first impression, but the impression that people have of you over time goes a long way. All of my clients, friends and family know that I do not curse or even yell. Let alone yell or curse at someone who was my father's age or the mayor of a city. I would never ever represent a client in an unprofessional manner. This was just not something I would do.

However, that's not to say that I don't speak up for myself. It may be difficult because I hate confrontation. I have always believed that your work speaks volumes and therefore you do not have to brag or boast about your abilities.

We were working for a financial client and they hired two public relations companies to get the word out about their product. This was easy for us as public relations is about relationships, and my background was so strongly entrenched within financial journalism for so long. I pitched the product to my colleagues, who were also my friends. While many publicists make cold calls, it is always easier to call on friends in anything we do. Since I had worked at Dow Jones and CNBC, I was calling on people I knew to cover my client. We got great coverage for this client. They were on CNBC and CNN, and in *Black Enterprise, Fortune, Forbes* and the *Wall Street Journal,* to mention a few. The problem came from the other PR company, as they wanted to take credit for my work. The male publicist wanted it to appear that he got *all* the media interviews, in particular the *Wall Street Journal* story. This was a lie. He stood before me and the client and stated this was his accomplishment. I didn't know what to do, but I knew I wasn't going to take it sitting down. The client replied that I had worked at Dow Jones, publisher of the *Wall Street Journal,* and he knew that I would not lie about the situation. I told the client he was correct. The other publicist still insisted he had secured the interview. But just to prove my point even further, I called the reporter and he sent a letter to the client saying that it was great having the interview set up by me.

Lesson learned—sometimes an impression may be that you are honest, but you may need supporting materials to back you up. It worked.

Chapter 7

Being Women in Business

Renée

The roles that men and women occupy in business are incessantly evolving. And so are the opinions about which roles women should play and how they should handle business situations. The roles women play around the world and throughout the country are so different. A "true southern" woman seems quite different from a northern woman but in many ways we are all the same. Kirsten and I have been friends for nearly two decades and oftentimes the more differences we appear to have the more similarities we actually have. I know that sounds so to the contrary, but it is so true. I think many of our core values from our parents are the same. And today we still believe in the same philosophy—work hard, trust in family and keep God in your life. We have always sought to be professional, which is a characteristic for both men and women—but the one thing that Kirsten and I truly were always on the same page about was that we weren't trying to be men in business, but good businesswomen. We embraced our sensitive, compassionate and feminine sides. We always tried to mix good sound business practices with our woman's intuition. In fact, when we haven't listened to our intuition or that inner voice, we've fallen short and inevitably something has gone awry.

Many times when we meet prospective clients, we have an initial gut reaction about whether they'll be difficult to work with or not. Initially, when we started our company, we took a few too many jobs because we felt we needed the business. We should have said no more often, but I was thinking of the bottom line. Kirsten "always" knew when a client would not suit us well. Today, we can somewhat pick and choose. There is not a situation when we don't see the writing on the wall. One example is a nonprofit we were working with for several years—from the first moment I met their new director, I knew that this would be our last year. After the initial meeting, I came back to the office and told Kirsten: "She doesn't like me, us—Noelle-Elaine—and we will not be working on this account much longer." After the event ended, the director indeed told us that this would be our last venture with them. Throughout the evening of the black-tie event, the director's incompetence, insecurities and just sheer lack of knowledge were apparent to all. Even basic principles weren't followed. Mayor Bloomberg attended the event, and my staff asked our photographer to follow the mayor, and this director informed me that we didn't need to do that because the mayor had a photographer with him. I insisted that we did because if we did not have our own photos, then we could not get one to the media. Anyone who has been in the public relations business would realize the mayor's photographer works for him and not our organization and it would take days to get them to send us a picture and by then it would not be news. Kirsten and I were always able to spot news and knew how to get our clients in the paper, and if the mayor was attending an event, that was a picture we could send to the style section of the *New York Times*.

We also knew that being women had its advantages and disadvantages. The advantages or benefits, we never turned down. For the past fifteen years since we have been in business, typically only one guy has worked for us at a time. It's not that we don't hire men, but typically more women apply for the positions or we are attracting more women. We get our testosterone from our events, which usually have lots of men in attendance—in fact, for a long time we worked for some very male-dominated firms and organizations. We didn't complain. All the women welcomed it—in fact, as single women we jumped for joy. We were traveling all over the country and world and would meet a variety of different men—it was always exciting.

In our office, because it was always women, when our service people would come to visit, they would oftentimes not even charge us. We would have technicians come into our office to fix the copier, fax machines, telephone lines—and they would actually think that we were "stupid." Okay, you're thinking to yourself, why would these smart women allow someone to think they were ignorant about the inner workings of the technology in their office? We weren't that stupid—in fact, we were pretty clever because we were watching the pennies and receiving free services. And the truth of the matter is that Kirsten or I, or even the office staff, didn't know anything about computers and welcomed the help. Of course, we could have read the manual, but we found our time better served sticking to planning events and discovering new venues to hold our next events. Different focus!

Over the years, Kirsten and I have trained so many young women to become great professionals. People who have worked with us are well established in their businesses. Our associates program trains young college students and graduates the basic principles of our business, and the more willing they are to learn, the more we will give them. We offer them an opportunity and they offer us affordable labor. We include them in our weekly staff meetings, assign them weekly assignments and tests and give them hands-on experience. A very bright young woman, Michelle Pascal, who started with us as an associate says it was the initial training she had from our company that allowed her to start her own firm. Today Michelle, president of MAP Unlimited, is still a part of our core team because we contract and partner with several other media relations firms. We trust her as a sister and professional woman with the same standards we believe in; it's at her core being. She is not alone; there are more than a dozen women who have started their firms because they said we gave them hope for success.

So, as the number of minority and women-owned businesses has increased, Kirsten and I feel like we are contributing to the growth of the American economy. We feel that as women, it is our personal responsibility to pass on our knowledge and insight to other young women. We are trying to "pay it forward."

According to data from the U.S. Census Bureau's 2002 Survey of Business Owners, minority groups and women are increasing their business ownership at a much higher rate than the national average. The number of U.S. businesses increased by 10 percent between 1997 and 2002, to 23 million. The rate of growth for minority- and women-owned businesses was far higher, ranging from 67 percent for native Hawaiian- and other Pacific islander-owned businesses to 20 percent for firms owned by women.

Firms owned by women of color now represent 21 percent of all privately held, majority-owned firms in the United States, and 29 percent of minority women-owned firms are owned by African Americans. African American women-owned firms employ 32 percent of the workers in African American-owned firms and generate 20 percent of the sales.

Kirsten and I feel that if we accomplish nothing else we will have given back by training other young women to be professionals. Now, while we have mentioned women who have started their own companies, hosts of other women say that we were the stepping-stone to other forms of success. Success varies for each person. For example, Carol Johnson Green is a successful booker who works with award-winning television personality Ed Gordon. Carol initially started with our company and for her, success was a job that would allow her more flexibility. At the start of our company, she was the lead on an account where she was introduced to Mr. Gordon and today she still works with him as his right-hand person. She has been married for nearly twenty years with two beautiful children—a true success story.

The keys to success are based on a combination of skills—integrity, negotiating and teamwork—and for Kirsten and me, it's been a sisterhood with hundreds of women from around the country. Ironically, we will have people who enter our office and are amazed that it's such a sisterhood, saying things like: "I can't believe you don't have fights." My comment is that employees only do what they see you do. The old saying that a fish stinks from his head—I think that's true. While we may disagree, we always respect one another and keep a calm head. In fact, nearly every employee past and present is our friend to this day and we go out socially with one another. We are a part of each other's history. When Kirsten got married five years ago, the entire office came. This wasn't out of obligation but out of sheer excitement and love for her. We partied all night.

It's about being authentic and I think as women in business, especially at Noelle-Elaine Media, we are authentic people.

That same authenticity extends across the continent. We have noticed that as women we are sometimes treated differently in other countries and we have to respect their traditions and still manage to get the job done. When we produced an international summit in Nigeria with thirty heads of state, including a U.S. presidential convoy, we had to take note. The protocol office of Nigeria was not used to women producing shows and serving in such an "out front" role. We had to manage to produce the event, not to disregard their tradition, and to be professional and get the job done. We did just that.

But in a situation, sometimes you don't have time to think, "If I were a man, this would not happen." Well, case in point, you're not a man, and you just have to find your way around the obstacles. From one extreme to the other—we have traveled to places where the men will not carry any box, bag or case. This is not a problem as we feel that we can manage it all. However, on a visit to Texas where we produced a one-day economic conference, the tide had turned. We were assisted and extended every southern hospitality there was. I can say: I love my southern men! Donna Stewart, our event manager, and I were setting up the economic conference and every time we turned around, there was a gentleman escort with us, *demanding* that we not lift a finger. It almost became debilitating as they were so much in front of us working. We felt like we needed to tip them, hire them or marry them.

As I said, I love my "southern men"—just add a little northern flair—perfect!

It was always important for Kirsten and me to be perceptive of when a male colleague was being chivalrous or patronizing. Our Texas boys were just being chivalrous, but we've had our share of men who were simply patronizing us and treated us in a way that conveyed "you just don't know what you're doing." Men who didn't want to pay us, berated us or just disrespected us. We didn't let that get in the way of us doing our jobs. We maintained our professionalism. When Kirsten and I planned several Caribbean soirees, one of the owners of the football team we were working with said to Kirsten that she had the "best legs in the Caribbean." Kirsten took the comment as a compliment and we continued to plan their celebration. But, clearly, that wasn't the most professional comment. You just have to know the boundaries and live within them and understand when it's a compliment.

Everything isn't a compliment. Sometimes our employees have overheard what they thought were clients "taking advantage" of us. The women in our company are very close. When one of our employees feels that a client is taking advantage of us as women or as a company—they become protective. I'm not sure if that would happen at an all-male company. But that's just fine with us.

There are many other differences that allow us to grow as a company. As a women-owned company, we are open to allowing our employees to work from home when necessary (to care for a sick child or on a day when schools are closed) or to bring their child into the office if the babysitter can't come in. We figure that we must all work together to get the job done. And we do!

When I had to have minor surgery and could not go into the office for more than two weeks, I was going stir-crazy and needed to work. I thought that Dr. Wenhui Jin was simply out of her mind when she told me that I would not be able to go back to work for that long. But she was correct, I could barely walk. Now the difference between an all-woman office and a male office is simple—past and present employees came to visit to ensure my sanity and health. In fact, Quamiesh McNeal, a young mother who is part of the glue that holds our office together, frequently stopped by to bring me work (this was work that I requested—yes, I wanted to work while recuperating). To this day, when she and her son pass my house, Aaron notes to his mom that "Miss Renée lives there."

Chapter 8

Tenacity

Kirsten

People ask how we have survived so many years and one word that keeps coming up is tenacity. When you work for yourself you find out what you are made of. And in addition to our livelihood, we are responsible for the livelihoods of others. If we fail, they are out of a job—and that is something we have never wanted on our heads. So we have always done what we needed to do and sometimes a little more.

One thing I learned from my old roommate Erica is that you keep asking the same question until someone gives you the answer you want—in other words, you never give up.

When I was graduating early from Syracuse, starting a full-time job the next month at a cable company while starting graduate school at the same time, I had to figure out a way to get it done. I worked during the day, did classes until ten at night and read my assignments on the hour-and-a-half ride back home—and actually did better in grad school than I did in college!

When my boss at CNBC, Brian, told me before I started that I had a week to learn a particular program on the computer, I had my girlfriend Tammi train me every night and came in ready to work. I also practiced commuting to the office, as it was in New Jersey and I had to figure out how to get there from the city before 9:00 a.m.—so I would try different routes. I remember the nights when I was so intimidated and tired from learning something new that I would work late trying to figure it out—my dad would pick me up from work and have pizza in the backseat to feed me, and Renée would come down and encourage me not to throw in the towel.

Brian was a Brooklyn boy, son of a detective—tough and smart as a whip. He would listen to rap, rock and Howard Stern and had a great rapport with reporters. At times I was afraid of him, but I would always thank him for giving me the chance to learn—and to cry. Like I said, I was often overwhelmed, but although we'd have our shouting matches, he would also let me close the door and cry in front of him when I was frustrated. I am sure he had his hands full with me—but that is what I needed to survive. I am so glad I had the tenacity to stick with it. I went from knowing nothing to getting two promotions in my two and a half years there, an invaluable learning experience.

I think that's part of the reason that Renée and I work so well together; it's because we always work and don't give up, and Renée will exhaust you with all that she takes on. When I think about what we created I think of that line from a Jay-Z track, "I'm not a businessman, I'm a business man!" We have always tried to figure out a way to get something done, even if our approach seemed a little unusual.

Before we left our full-time jobs at CNBC, we had a business trip in Venezuela for a new client who was hosting a conference in Caracas. I knew basic Spanish, but when I called the media over the phone I was "lost in translation." I even had my Spanish-speaking intern do a few calls for me, but as she was an intern, she could not exactly pitch the project for me. Finally, we asked our client to just send us there—we would just try to meet with the media upon arrival.

We got to Caracas armed with a media list and their addresses, got in a taxi and showed up, unannounced, at each media outlet. I knew enough to say in broken Spanish, "I am sorry, I speak very little Spanish. I am from the United States and my client is a businessman who wants to talk with your boss about a business meeting in Caracas. Do you have anyone who speaks English?" That seemed to do the trick! They were so impressed that we had just flown down there, and happy that we respected them enough to attempt (although poorly) to speak in their language, that we got into every single door and got coverage from all the papers. The funny thing is, Renée was taking a Spanish beginners course and she understood their responses better than I did. I was spending so much energy trying to think of the right words to say that when I was done speaking, I could not listen. So I talked and she listened! We were a great team from the beginning.

The event turned out to be a bust because, once again, the client did not listen to our suggestions for getting the Caracas business community out—they just wanted us to stay in our box and do media. So hardly anyone showed up—but we did get great preevent coverage. And, boy, did we have a great time in Venezuela—we spent our off time going to the beach and shopping and basically working on our tans. I tell you, we also survived because we knew how to throw in fun.

Somehow in those early years, we were always in the middle of an international event that required us to deal with language barriers, social barriers, etc. We once worked for a Paris-based Internet company that served as a resource for musicians and the music community. My friend Eric Liley, who I met by arguing with him over a sponsor banner years before, started work with this company and hired our firm for PR and events. They were planning simultaneous launch parties in New York and Paris and we were hired to produce both events as well as to conduct a live webcast between the two cities. Mind you, this was the nineties and webcasting wasn't as simple as it is today—I felt like we were trying to send a man to the moon!

Because headquarters were in Paris I got to go there for the first time. It was so interesting to be in an office where everyone could smoke. We were there for a week and would go into meetings where the conference room would be filled with smoke. As a nonsmoker, it was a bit difficult, but hey, I was in their country and they had the right to live and work as they wanted. While there, we also managed to have fun. Danielle and I took the opportunity to tour the city—we had a little spot where we bought croissants each morning before work. We stayed at a hotel right near the Louvre and were centrally located. We went to the Eiffel Tower, rode the merry-go-round, shopped on the Champs-Élysées, went out to clubs, restaurants and bars with the Paris-based team and even went to a concert. Paris was such a beautiful city, one I would visit again in the future as part of my honeymoon. And it was so easy to get around. We just hopped on a train and were off! I could not believe that this was my life—flying around the world, planning international events.

But it wasn't so simple. Paris was not as up to speed with technology as we were, and a week before the event, we learned that although its staff had told us it was wired for Internet service, the venue was actually wired for phone service. Unlike in New York, you could not make an appointment and get service the next day—it typically took a month. We didn't have a month—we had one week before we were going live, so we needed to speak with French Telecom immediately. Fortunately, when Renée and I were on a business trip to Ghana about a year before, we did a side vacation to the Ivory Coast, where she made friends with a French business-man we met on the beach. They stayed in contact and luckily he was able to intercede on our behalf as our consultant and served as our Paris liaison. Christian negotiated everything for us. Our clients had to compromise and pay for the venue to get wired, which was not cheap, but they had no choice. And because money talks, it was finished before showtime. Danielle and our freelancer, Kim Hudson, were already in-country to find the bands that would perform and to manage the event on-site.

On the New York end, we were running around trying to find trendy furniture to fill the venue we'd selected as well as to find a company that could service the live webcast. We had a live perfor-mance from (the now late) Grover Washington, Jr., that would be fed to Paris; a band at the club in Paris that would perform live; and live remarks from company heads in both cities. With a six-hour time difference it was important that we start on time. Grover was traveling from another performance and we literally had minutes to go live. I always say "God likes Noelle-Elaine" because somehow we pulled it all off and it went off without a hitch.

There were so many entities involved but all we could see was the end goal. The late and great humanitarian and civil rights leader Leon H. Sullivan, whose foundation was also our client, always said, "I see no mountains," and that is the attitude you have to have going into this business—you can't see obstacles, you have to keep moving forward.

And moving forward is what Renée did when we were shooting that documentary in Africa. The client wanted to get a quote from Nelson Mandela, but we could not get a confirmation. Renée went in-country with a camera crew to tape the other parts of the documentary, but while there found out Mandela's schedule and went to every event he attended in an effort to get him to do an interview. Every time she would try to get close, the security guards would push her back—I am sure they thought she was a crazy woman. But after the third attempt or so, she got a chance to speak with him and he agreed to do a one-on-one interview right there on the spot! All of that persistence led to a Telly Award, so it was worth the effort. The funny thing is, when she returned to the United States, there was a form letter on her desk from his office, apologizing and saying they would not be able to accommodate the interview request!

What I love about Renée is that she never takes no for an answer—she keeps pushing the envelope. I even remember once while we were working at CNBC, we went out for lunch, and on our way back to the office, a police car with his siren on was trying to get past us. There was a car in front of us and a car in front of him so we literally could not move. The police officer was irate—so irate that I am convinced that if we were men (and, God forbid, black men), we would have been in jail or worse. He came stomping and screaming out of the car, yelling at us for not getting out of the way. Renée jumped out of the car to explain the situation (we had never been stopped before so we did not know that you are supposed to stay in your car). Every vein in this man's head was popping and he continued to berate us for not moving, while writing a ticket (so much for the emergency he was headed to—probably lunch). Renée kept trying to explain her case and even then we were an unknowing tag team because while she was talking and he was yelling, I was for once the calm one, sitting there writing down his name and badge number. When we got back to CNBC, she naturally had to explain why she was late. Fortunately, an anchor that Renée worked with named Ted David heard what happened and immediately picked up the phone, called the police chief and explained our side of the story, giving the chief the officer's name and number. He then added, "And I don't think it was a coincidence that these were two black women." Needless to say we got an apology and we did not get a ticket! But I admired the way Renée kept going and insisting that the officer hear her point of view—even when he was a lunatic. And although Ted David did not really know me from Adam, I am thankful that he took the time to intervene on our behalf.

That tenacity paid off again when she found out that James Earl Jones was staying at the very hotel where we were doing an event.

Again, we were trying to get him to participate in this documentary on Africa. Crazy Renée actually called the man's room, got him on the phone and had a conversation with him. He was kind enough to listen and said he would have to consider it but was getting ready to leave the hotel. So Renée waited in the lobby with the bellman until she saw him come downstairs and introduced herself. He actually complimented her on her persistence and promised he'd follow up. Although he was unable to participate, he was gracious enough to listen and hear her out—and respond.

Sometimes we are thrown into situations where we are not prepared and still have to make it happen. I was at a film festival in Acapulco where I was supposed to handle media for a client. However, when I got there, I learned that their producer couldn't make it, so I ended up having to wrangle celebrities and get them to come over for a minute and do interviews. It's amazing the clout and fearlessness you have with a camera! I had to literally walk up to people in midconversation, introduce myself, tell them who I represented and convince them to stop what they were doing to do an interview with me on the spot. I would catch celebrities talking to their friends or going into or out of a screening, and I'd have to just walk up with a microphone in my hand and get the interview. In some cases, if we did not physically see a person, I just used a little ingenuity. I'd call the most expensive hotel in Acapulco—because you can believe, nine times out of ten, that's where they were staying—and leave a message in their rooms. Although I felt like a stalker, I got nearly every single interview I went after—with no experience— and everyone was pleasant and gracious and cooperative.

Sometimes I wasn't so lucky. When trying to interview a model turned businesswoman for a project, I was having a hard time getting an answer from her office, so I showed up with a bunch of flowers to convince her to do an interview. She was not there and her associate was none too pleased that I showed up unannounced, so she took the flowers out of my hand with an annoyed (or maybe it was incredulous) "thanks" and firmly showed me the door. But I must have made some impression, as she did pass on my information. Although the woman could not do the project, I give her credit for following up with what must have appeared to be a crazy woman at her door.

I think one of our best moments, when we were thinking, "Damn, we really do know what we are doing," was when we did a dinner where George W. Bush was being honored. Throughout the early stages of planning, we were constantly meeting with his security detail, working out the logistics of the dinner and making adjustments to suit their requirements. We knew that hotel like the back of our hand and were able to offer sound suggestions that they incorporated into their detail. But one thing they made clear— President Bush had to go on at a certain time and leave at a certain time and regardless of what else was going on, we had to hit that mark, as he had to leave for the next event.

I was working the VIP reception where the president was and then had to coordinate private photo ops. Of course everyone wanted a photo with him and he was kind and friendly and down-to-earth. He accommodated everyone that we gave clearance to—which of course took time. Renée was in the other room literally having to start the show. She was dealing with the production, the dancers who were opening the show and literally starting the program. I had to trust that she was doing what she had to do in one room while she had to trust that I would get the president out of that reception and photo op with enough time to get on the stage for his remarks. All we had were cell phones with bad connections—but by the time I escorted the president's team to the stage, they were introducing him. He went right up, gave his remarks and left, and his team parted with a "Wow, you guys really know what you are doing!" I consider that an official seal of approval.

Other times, we had to be demanding. We were working with actors from a commercial that became a national and international craze and were on the road with them doing media and promotional events all over the country—the *Today* show, *The Tonight Show, E! All Star Weekend*—we were all over the place. During one particular media tour, the brand that was represented in the commercial wanted me to take a backseat as their brand manager was handling things; I was merely representing the ad agency that worked with the man who had created the commercial. Right away I clearly saw that this guy did not know what he was doing. In his defense, he was a marketing guy, not a PR guy, and there is a difference. So he was lost when it came to media. That was confirmed when we went to a radio station. The promo department wanted them to do a promo that I felt was questionable and would jeopardize not only the guy's reputation, but the brand as well. But I sat still and waited to see what the brand manager would do—which was nothing. He let them record the promo and laughed all the way through it.

After it was recorded I went to the promo manager at the station and explained why I thought the promo was a bad move for the guys, the brand and their station and that they should not air the promo, no matter how catchy it was. He agreed with me; but before I left, I asked for the original of the recording—and he gave it to me. I did not want there to be any chance that that promo would make air. I was so glad that I went over the brand manager's head. These were nice guys who were having the experience of a lifetime—this promo could have caused an uproar and ruined everything.

Other times, even when we didn't want to be so tenacious, it paid off that we were. We had heard that a legendary music artist was looking for a new PR firm. Once again, a good opening conversation that I had was the key to our opportunity. We actually were looking to work with a company designing the artist's Web site. They ended up not being able to hire us—but knew the artist was looking for a firm and recommended us. We sent them information and waited, and nothing happened. Finally, it was Christmas Eve and we were closing up the office, trying to get out the door, when the phone rang. The artist wanted to make an announcement about his disagreement with his label. We did everything to try to convince the people calling that this was a bad time to make an announcement, it was the end of the day, a holiday, and it would get buried. Everyone knows that when you have to make an announcement but you want it to get buried or you want to prevent the hype, you do it over a long weekend or a holiday.

They did not care and basically said, "This is your shot; if you want the job, do it." We had never personally represented an artist before so we weren't sure what to do, but we knew we had better come up with something. So we thought about what was the best way to get the news out (again, this was before the Internet craze).

We decided on the Associated Press, because if the release was picked up it would go out across the country, and on the news department at MTV News, which would spread the word to the entertainment community. I think they were literally the only media outlets that we pitched—we were still trying to get home and enjoy the holiday—but it worked. The artist's team called us back and said that he had seen himself on the news that same night and hired us because we made it happen. We only worked with the artist for less than a year (from our understanding, that was about the average length he kept firms), but it was a once-in-a-lifetime experience. He was a genius and an entrepreneur that the music industry tried to paint as crazy. But he was ahead of his time—he was one of the first, if not the first, to demand that he own the rights to his music and to release music when and how he wanted to, and he was one of the first to begin selling his own music over the Internet. So I say he was "crazy like a fox"—he started what has become standard with artists in the music industry today—and those ten or eleven months were invaluable.

We have always gone the extra mile, for better or worse. We have started projects that ended up being way more than we signed up for—and completed them. We always knew that our names and reputation were on the line, so we could never give it less than our best.

But like I have said, sometimes giving your best is not enough. We have often been the "bridesmaid" when pitching big business. One time we pitched a big account while I was on vacation. They had changed the meeting date but I was not about to miss this opportunity; this was a relationship I had nurtured for over a year, since meeting someone from the company at a reception, and I was so happy that we were going to get our chance.

The company had two small agencies and two large agencies pitching the business. We had to find a Kinko's where I could "go live" while Renée was on-site. We gave a good presentation and really felt confident that we had the business, especially after so many people came up to Renée afterward and said what a good job we had done. But we did not get the business—they ended up going with a larger agency with proven contacts in the African American community. The same ones that we had, as it happened, but apparently they were wise enough to spend their time explaining these relationships while we spent our time explaining our experience.

The good thing that came out of this, however, was that the client took the time to explain what we could have done better, so it was a great learning experience—and they hired us later to work on another project. It was not nearly as lucrative, but it gave us the chance to get our foot in the door and was the beginning of what I think will be a long relationship.

Another time, Renée and Danielle flew to Chicago for a big pitch when we didn't have the money. Again, we put together what we thought was a dynamic presentation, but because we had not worked in that industry before, they just could not see how we could do the work. They didn't take into account that everything we had done before—with success—was new to us, until someone gave us a chance. Plus, when you understand the media, you understand the media. It is expected that you are comfortable or at least knowledgeable about pitching various types of media. We were an agency, for goodness' sake—pitching different accounts and working on different projects was something we did every day. First book tour: *New York Times* bestseller list. First hair company we worked with: *Good Morning America, E! Entertainment*, MTV, *Teen People, Seventeen, Essence*, and a "Kiss of Approval" from *CosmoGirl!* magazine. The first time we did an investor's survey we were in all of the major papers. We know how to make something happen!

But nothing could make this client believe that we could do the work. Same with a large computer company; they were wary because of our small staff—we would have to hire additional staff to do the work and they were worried about our ability to get up to speed, while the company they hired already had the staff in place.

But everything happens for a reason. I knew at our pitch meeting how much work that account was going to be. It was an account that I felt would demand long hours and work on weekends and holidays. I prayed to God, "Please, if this account is going to change our lifestyle in a drastic way, don't let us get the business." I was concerned about how that particular account would affect our lifestyle and office environment. And we didn't get the business.

Although at times I feel we have not been hired because of our size, I have to think that we work on the accounts that we are supposed to work on and those that we are ready for. While it is always our goal to get the "big business," everyone gets the best we have to offer and we can go to bed at night knowing we did our job.

We were already working hard and each year always brought a few new projects for us to work on—we were busy enough. So busy that we did not realize until it was too late that we were clearly not minding the shop!

Chapter 9

A Taxing Time

Kirsten

I knew I'd get married later in life. Maybe I needed more time to figure things out; maybe I needed more time to be sure of who I was and what I wanted. I just always knew that I never experienced "it"—when you just know that you are going to spend the rest of your life with someone.

A few years before I met my husband, Larry, we had an intern who, for lack of a better word, was psychic. She just had a gift for seeing into the future and, with an office full of women, we all, at one point or another, booked a session with her. Like all the other women in the office, I asked about relationships. I was in my thirties and wondering when and if I'd ever be married. I was starting to doubt my own intuition that it would happen. She told me that I would meet my husband in three years (which at the time seemed like an eternity). She said that I would meet someone else first and that he would be a great guy, extremely athletic and we'd really

143

like each other—but he wasn't the one and it wasn't going to work out. It wouldn't be either of our faults; he just wouldn't be "it."

She said my husband was all around me and that, although I hadn't met him yet, she was surprised because we were literally in the same places. She said he'd love me incredibly hard and that we'd both know that we were meant to be in each other's lives; that we wouldn't have a long courtship and would marry rather quickly. Although disappointed that I still had to wait three years, I was pretty confident that I'd have a happy ending; so it was worth the wait.

Sure enough, on assignment for an entertainment cable TV client in Acapulco I found out that I had to wrangle celebrities for interviews that would air because their producer couldn't make the trip. And then I saw the cameraman. I had scouted him on the bus from the airport the night before and thought he was extremely hot. When I learned my assignment the next morning, they said, "And here is your cameraman"—and in he walked. Six foot four, from California; laid-back and cute. We worked and hung out all weekend and I just knew he was the one for me. We made plans to stay in touch. He played basketball in college for a major university, skied, snowboarded, mountain biked; he lived in the mountains in California and spent his days as a cameraman for another entertainment network and had been freelancing with my client when we met. We dated, met each other's parents, talked late nights on the phone, but sure enough in six months it was over. I had had the "it" conversation with him. I told him I didn't see "it" in us; I thought it was something we could work toward but he apparently agreed with my assessment and bailed.

That was a hard one. In your twenties you go through the breakups and makeups with relative ease, but by the time you're in your thirties your heart is weary from the cycle of healing and hurting so frequently. So I simply decided to stop dating. Why not take a break before I lost all faith in the fact that I was a great gal who would definitely be married. For about three years I just hung out with my friends and with myself. Eventually, I put my toe back in the water and met a record producer about eight years my junior. I also flirted with an old crush from college. But both men seemed to think I had time to wait around for them to make plans with me. My self-confidence and good sense weren't going to let that happen.

Soon after, I was in Washington, D.C., planning a co-ed baby shower for my dear friend Lisa Hew and her husband, Karl. Karl had a friend he wanted me to meet. To be honest, Lisa wanted to put the kibosh on it, saying that he seemed very nice—he just didn't talk. She wasn't sure how well that was going to fit with my personality. I was too busy working and ignoring him at the shower but finally, through my sister and brother-in-law's intervention, I met the man who would be my husband. Of course I did not recognize him at the time. I always thought I'd marry "Michael Jordan" lookswise, but this guy was more a young "Smokey Robinson"—also good looking, but completely opposite of what I expected. Fortunately he was persistent, for a quiet man. We talked all afternoon after we met; we liked a lot of the same things and he loved New York—which is what I really liked about him—he was funny, an entertainment junkie like me, and had a smart-ass sense of humor, like me. He planned for us to catch up the next day but I never called because my grandmother, who by now had been living in D.C. for years, was very ill.

I returned to New York and continued dating casually. I was on fire and certainly wasn't thinking about settling down with one man. But Larry kept calling and e-mailing. He even came to New York (uninvited) with Lisa and Karl so that we could get to know each other more.

At the time I did not get his (many) messages saying he was headed into town, so when Lisa told me he was literally in the car with her I said, "Well, you can tell him that if he wants to go on a date with me, he should call and ask me out and I'll see if I'm available." Only after getting his messages, and Lisa begging me, did I agree to meet them for dinner. At the beginning I just wasn't sure. A true romantic, Larry says he knew at first sight that I was the one. One of his favorite songs as a kid was "Endless Love," but he called me his "ambivalent love" because I would just not respond to him and I have to admit, I was not letting him in. I was enjoying going out with guys and not taking it seriously. I had a saying, "Every man you date is either going to be your ex-boyfriend or your husband. All but one will end up in the ex category, so don't take it so seriously." I knew, knew, knew that I was onto something with this theory, but I just did not see it banging on my door. I had such an image of what my husband would look like that I did not realize that this handsome man had, more important, everything I needed my husband to *feel* like.

Eventually my grandmother passed away. I still wasn't returning his calls too often so I finally told him what had happened—and he wrote me the most beautiful e-mail about when his great-grandmother died and how they were close and how he was so happy to have spent time with her. He wanted to know if he could see me when I came back down for the funeral. It had been about two weeks since we met. Before the doorbell rang, I had just said to my aunt, "Isn't love supposed to hit you over the head? I mean, I'm getting ready to go out with this guy and he's nice and all, but I'm just doing it to have something to do. If he never called me again, I think I'd be cool with that; I'm so busy with everyone else." And then the door opened and in he walked and every bell in my head went off. The man was "fresh pressed," as they used to say—I mean groomed to the hilt—and he came with flowers for me, and a sympathy card for my family. And the complete joy at seeing me, and the sincerity for my family, was written all over his face—and it just got me. I still remember the outfit he was wearing and see the look in his eyes when he saw me. It was like he came in with a glow around him, as if God was saying "This is him, idiot!" He met the entire side of my mother's family with ease and as we left to go out to dinner that night I remember turning around and seeing my aunts, my mom and my uncles and just having a big grin on my face as I said, "Bye!" The next day, he even found out where the funeral was, and without telling me, went to pay his respects. My brother-in-law joked that he was probably already in West Virginia, where we buried my grandmother, polishing the casket and digging the grave!

I knew then and there that this was "it." This was what I was talking about—someone just getting me and knowing what I needed and knowing how to give it to me. Larry and I were engaged ten months later and married six months after that. And yes, we found out he was indeed all around me. We were both in Lisa and Karl's wedding—even in the same picture—but we never met; he had come with them to one of my movie screenings—and we never met; we were even on the same boat ride and never met. But we did finally meet, as my intern said, three years from the time she predicted we would!

It may sound weird, but Larry is like the combination of all of my girlfriends rolled into one. More important, he reminds me of my sister, sometimes acts like my father (their birthdays are a day apart) and sees eye to eye with my mother—all people whom I love dearly. Down-to-earth, funny, fun, sincere, real. Or maybe I am just free to be myself with him—a comfort level I've only had in the past with other women and family. I mean, I think I'm a pretty regular girl. I've been told that I'm attractive, but have always been more complimented when someone told me I was smart. I'm not into makeup and having my hair perfectly coiffed all the time—when I can get away with it, I wash and go. I can't put on a pretense of happiness when I feel like crap. I can't pretend I like you when I don't and I don't believe in running around in fancy underwear, heels and pearls to try to get a man. I love having flaws. I love that it's my wit that will attract you, not what I'm wearing. Like my sister always says, "All the women running around in fake maid's uniforms and a feather duster are single and all the women in big white panties are married." In other words, the right kind of man appreciates a woman who's comfortable in her own skin.

That's what Larry was for me—validation that I was not crazy. That when I used to sit at night and ask God to reveal the person he wanted me to be with, I was not talking to thin air. That I was not insane to expect not just a handsome, educated single man with no children—all of which he was—but a person with a soul and a sincerity that would rock me to my core. That's what grabbed me about Larry—his heart. He's by nature a quiet guy but he was bold in his love for me, which allowed for me to be bold right back. I was not afraid to say that I was looking for a relationship that would lead to marriage; that I will not date you if you are not in the same place, but I will love you fiercely if you are. And he accepted all of that and more.

I'm not necessarily easy to get along with—I'm opinionated, high-strung, smart-mouthed with a bad temper. My girlfriend Dana and I used to go to Barnes and Noble at Lincoln Center and pull out all of these books on astrology and relationships as we tried to figure out our lives. I ran across a description of my sign, Aries, as "intense." I said to her, "I'm not intense." She looked at me, stunned, and said, "Kirsten, you're intense about a peanut butter and jelly sandwich."

But Larry just got me—he knew exactly where I was coming from and from the minute we met, he had no doubt that I was the one for him. More important, he wasn't afraid to show it. I never doubted how he felt about me—he was never too cool to meet me halfway and he was patient when my hot temper would send me over the edge.

Although I grew up in New York and Larry in Maryland, we had very similar middle-class upbringings. We're both one of two siblings, except he's the oldest—important because I could maintain my "baby" status. He did the Catholic school thing, attending an all-boys high school in Maryland, and went to a historically black college in Virginia, where he developed close lifelong friend-ships. He chose the state law school that accepted him rather than be wait-listed at the more prestigious law school, knowing that the move would save him thousands of dollars. Like me, he's been in business for himself for over ten years. In addition to building up a nice business, he was solid and practical. He'd owned his own home since law school, paid for his car in full and didn't believe in big bills or big debt—which would come in handy later. He'd been in love before—he was actually engaged to a woman who had the same birthday as me! Although it didn't work out, I saw this as a plus—he was able and willing to commit to someone; and when it didn't work out, he was able to be a decent human being about it. I never heard him utter a negative word about her, which showed me he was respectful.

Larry also came from a happily married two-parent household, which was a big plus for me. I always felt that there was something a person would pick up by osmosis just seeing two people work together on solving their problems. In those early arguments we had when we were getting to know each other, I'd be ready to walk and he'd be ready to rationalize. I remember once after we had been dating a few months and I was moving closer to buying a house and had committed to the D.C. area, we had gotten into an argument. In my outrage, I jumped up, pulled on my clothes and said I was going back to New York—in the middle of the night. I called my sister and she simply said, "Kirsten, you're buying a house. What do you mean you're going home? You *are* home in D.C.—get back in bed." What she and Larry saw was this was it, this was not a game, this was not something you could throw a tantrum at and leave, this was life—figure it out. And that was Larry—always ready to figure it out.

Now don't get me wrong—we have argued and continued to argue. I get mad and the mouth comes out, he gets mad and the steely silence comes out. But it's never for long and we both always know that it's temporary. But back then we were still figuring things out.

I loved that we could have the best day in the world just going to a park or hunkering down all day and watching movies. I loved that he had his own life with his friends—ski trips, football games, cigar nights—he had his own core of good friends who loved him fiercely and his own support system. He didn't need me. He wasn't looking for me to complete his life. I just complemented it. At Christmas I met his entire family—aunts, cousins, grandmother, great-aunts, you name it. I loved that he had a big welcoming family. His mother had already shared my company Web site with everyone and she and his dad were immediately embracing. Those first few months were full of holidays and surprise parties—I threw one for him, he threw one for me—and all of our friends and families got to know each other.

One night in June, somewhere between *Sex and the City* and *The Wire*, he proposed to me. I knew it was coming. As a matter of fact, I had written in my diary that I had a feeling that something was going to happen soon. Not to mention that when we first started dating and he told me he still had his ex-fiancée's engagement ring after two years because he didn't know what to do with it, I took him to a friend's family jeweler, who promptly sold it. I already had in the back of my head that he would use that money as a down payment for my ring—and he would purchase it at that very place! Ever the romantic, he planned to propose at a concert we were going to in Prospect Park since that was where we had our first New York date, but it was rained out. The poor guy had no choice but to feign an excuse to get me downstairs so he could drop to one knee and propose. Although I knew it was coming, I was stunned. He claims I said, "What are you doing?!" and grabbed the ring and put it on my finger without answering! I was just in shock—we were in a stairway, of all places, so I just couldn't connect the two! Despite what he claims, I said yes!

So when my wedding came, it was an extremely good time in my life. I was not nervous or anxious. I just knew I was marrying the man I was meant to spend the rest of my life with; and I had been in business with one of my best friends for eleven years and all was right with the world.

Everything was paid, both the wedding and the honeymoon. We had no debt. Because I hired people that I trusted and had worked with for years, I had no problems paying everyone in advance—the photographer, the DJ, the hair stylist, the makeup artist. All were paid and tipped before I walked down the aisle. I did not want to have to dig in my purse the day of my wedding. I knew that I was on the right path with everything, both personally and professionally. On the day of my wedding, I was calm. Our photographer said that she had never seen a bride fall asleep the day of her wedding (she took a picture of it); but I was so sure about every step I was about to take. The wedding was everything we hoped for. My dear uncle Donald married us and we partied the rest of the night with 140 of our friends and family. The next day we left for a two-week honeymoon in Paris and Mauritius and came back tanned and relaxed.

I still hadn't figured out how I was going to be married in two cities and run a business in New York. We even flew back to New York after the honeymoon and I stayed to work and Larry went back home! We were used to dating long distance so I think for a while I pretended marriage wouldn't change a thing. Once I gave up my carriage house apartment in Brooklyn that I loved, I simply moved three blocks away with my sister, her husband and my nephew. Almost immediately after Dee and Fred had started dating, he moved in with us into our duplex on the Upper East Side. Although we all got along great, I used to tell Dee that he needed to start paying rent; payback was a bitch because now here I was living with them—and not paying rent—but I did help out with my gorgeous nephew Evan a lot!

I just didn't want to abandon the office. We were small, we were all women, and we were all close. How would I know if they were having a bad day? How would I know if I was calling in the middle of a crisis? How would I know if they needed me? Was I putting an unfair burden on them? I wasn't too worried about our clients. A lot of the work we did was outside of New York, so they were used to operating with us by phone and e-mail. But the business was my baby, something I helped create, something I had helped build.

It was Renée who convinced me that it would be okay and that it really wasn't a big deal. She loved New York, always knew she'd live there and planned on staying there. I always felt that I'd get married and leave New York—I just didn't factor in the "own my own business" part. We always worked on separate accounts—I on the business I brought in, she on the business she brought in; the employees split the workload and we'd all get together at event time. In our naïveté, I don't think either of us was thinking about the operations part—after all, we had our accountant who handled that. Renée said it would be easy.

But a part of me also feared that being away would reveal how much I wasn't needed. I wasn't the energetic personality Renée was. I didn't necessarily want to be friends with my clients. If it happened naturally, cool, but I didn't want anyone calling me after work or on weekends asking me to do work, unintentionally taking advantage because we were "friends." I personally felt Renée did too much of that, always overextending herself for a client—even for her friends—and I felt it was wearing her out. But still, she always seemed on the go, juggling ten things at once, always working late and on weekends, always moving. I felt guilty that she was always so busy, but I had to get comfortable with the fact that that was not the life I wanted and that it was okay.

Carol Green's words came back to haunt me—in a good way. In addition to being our friend, Carol had worked with us when we first started. After about a year she decided that it was too much trying to juggle being our employee, a good wife and a good mother and that she needed to find something more flexible. Subsequently she became a sought-after booker and producer—all from the comfort of her home, all while being able to teach aerobics and pick her kids up from school. She had created the life that she wanted. She built it and they came. So one day on the phone, she told me to just live the life I wanted and it started to click: I could live in two cities. I realized that I was already starting to build it—I didn't want the madness of running ten accounts, my four were bringing in just as much money—and I had time to rest, to sleep, to have my weekends and it was okay. Just because I wasn't running around did not mean I wasn't contributing. We were different women with different styles of doing things; we did not have to be mirror images of each other.

So slowly, I started staying with Larry more. I had my office set up in the basement. I was focused. I didn't have to deal with the phones ringing, the deliveries or the confused interns; I could just work on my shit. I had my little area set up and was quite proud that I never turned on the TV. I'd get up, shower, eat, read the paper and get right down to work, seldom leaving the desk before Larry got home. As a matter of fact, I had to make it a rule that we would always kiss each other before he left for work and I'd always drag myself off of the computer to greet him when he got home—or else I'd fear I'd disappear into the black hole. I was so focused working from there that I knew if I didn't get dressed that morning it might not ever happen—once I hit the basement, I was locked in my seat and on the phone and computer. I was still going back and forth but at least my new house was starting to feel more like home.

Things were great. I had a system, a plan. My sister and I were never asked if we wanted to go to college—it was more "Where are you going to college?" My parents were both college educated so it was assumed we'd follow the plan—and we did. This too was part of the plan: Get a career? Check. Work hard? Check. Fall in love with the right man (finally)? Check. Run a business? Check. Get married? Check. The system was working—and then the phone rang. It was Renée. And it was not good.

As you may have already figured out, Renée is the eternal optimist. I am not. I have this theory about women (yes, I had a concentration in psychology in college). Those whose parents were divorced and had no relationship, or a bad one, with their father are more pessimistic in their outlook. Those whose parents were divorced, but who had a good relationship with their father, are pretty middle of the road, sometimes optimistic, some times real downers. I considered myself in this category. But those whose parents were happily married are the eternal glass-half-full people. It's worked that way across the board for every woman that I have known. And although I sometimes think the optimists are a little removed from reality and don't always see a situation for what it truly is, I have relied on their outlook to pull me through. Renée was my optimist; my "we can do it"; my "don't put it out there" if a bad thought came to mind, as if ignoring it could wish it away. She was Mary Tyler Moore to my Rhoda Morgenstern. So when she called and sounded like the blood was literally being drained from her body, I knew something was wrong.

I had been married for about six weeks. I was doing my home-with-husband shift and in one instant my life seemed to go from endless possibilities to seemingly endless disaster. It was a gorgeous day and Renée was about to close on a condo that she had found at a great price in Harlem. She had an excellent deal on her mortgage and was days away from making the home her own when the bank called and informed her that she could not close on the home because there was a lien against her and she owed over $100,000 in taxes. She knew this was a mistake; she didn't owe anybody anything. Then she found it wasn't her personally, but our company, and that as an officer of the company she was liable.

We didn't know what was happening until we spoke to our accountant and the pieces slowly started to fall into place. To put it simply, Renée and I had not paid our payroll taxes—for a few years. We knew we weren't paying them but did not realize the implications.

We had been in business for about six years when we met our accountant. We agreed to hire him and he slowly started taking over our books, our bookkeeping, our taxes, etc. We were a small business and, to be honest, we were relieved that someone was handling all the bills and finances. We figured that as long as we were signing the checks, nothing could happen to us. Slowly but surely he started telling us that we had no money, that we had to lay off employees if we were going to survive. At the time there were about twelve of us; we reduced our staff to five—but he still claimed that we had no money. And yet, he never produced evidence. He never produced profit-and-loss statements. He never showed us our monthly expenses—he just said we didn't have it.

I am embarrassed to admit how easily we listened to him but at the time we were running around making a cardinal mistake— taking care of our clients instead of taking care of our business. Renée and I would spend hours working on client accounts, traveling, conducting meetings, working on events, anything to keep the client happy. But we had stopped talking about our business. It was always put on the back burner in support of the people who were paying us.

We had stopped having partner retreats, we stopped looking at where we were and where we needed to go—we were just operating day-to-day and letting the accountant worry about the bills. We stopped looking at the financial health of the company. We didn't want the stress of dealing with it, and when the accountant begged off of having a meeting with us, as he often did, we were too tired to fight.

Eventually he suggested that we cancel our contract with our payroll company and let him do our payroll. He stated that we didn't have the money every two weeks to pay taxes so why not just let him print all the checks, and we'd pay our employees and then pay the taxes when the money came—which, according to him, never did. Again, we agreed. He said he would handle the IRS agents, who, over the years, started to call—and visit—and ask questions. But he claimed he had it under control—and every time they called, we called him and considered it done.

Soon he was lending us money—which added more to the confusion—we never knew what we owed him and what we were paying him back for. In addition he was charging us his $150 an hour accountant's rate when he was doing things (or not doing things) like bookkeeping and paying our bills. The funny thing is, when it all came out in the wash, he never actually did accounting. He never filed extensions with the IRS, never filed our taxes and never entered into discussions with them on our behalf. So by the time they got their hands on Renée, they were treating us like criminals.

We did not realize the ramifications of our actions—it's not that we weren't paying taxes; we weren't paying payroll taxes, which meant we weren't paying into our own or our employees' Social Security taxes, FICA, etc. We were technically stealing from their futures—leaving them with nothing should we go out of business. We had no idea that we were on the verge of ruining people's lives.

So many things were spinning in my head. How did this happen? What the hell happened? Why did it happen to her and not me? I thought back to when we first started the company.

I had always somehow managed to avoid personal disaster. It was a running joke that I always preceded disaster, or I was in it or around it but never really affected by it. This seemed to be true. I was in the big Northridge earthquake that hit California. I was actually there for work in Pasadena at the TV Critics Tour. My hotel room was at the Ritz Carlton, but I was hanging with my girlfriend in Inglewood. We went out to the Roxy and danced all night with plans to go to the Martin Luther King, Jr., Day parade the next morning. So I stayed at her house and was there when the earthquake hit. Inglewood, or at least where she lived, was barely touched. I was in two national airline strikes—one in Jamaica and one in Venezuela. Both happened when we were at the airport to return to the States. I had already had my vacation, so I was cool! In Jamaica we even met a guy on line who went to college with a guy whose mom owned a hotel there. So while everyone else was crying and fighting in the airport, we were chilling at a hotel, having drinks and playing in the pool. Brazil? Mechanical failure forced the plane to stay a night in São Paulo. Again, I had just spent ten days in Rio and Bahia—what was another night in Brazil? In Puerto Rico, Renée and I had our partners' retreat when a huge hurricane hit—on our last day. We had already had our fun; we stayed an extra night and got out in the morning. So I had a feeling I could avoid disasters.

So when I looked back at my journals, I was not surprised to see that a week into discovering the madness, my initial reaction was relief. I still believed that we would find a way out of this—that Renée would help us find a way out of this—I needed her optimism. Before "the call," Renée and I just knew something was up with the accountant but we were too tired to try to figure out what. The IRS situation put a name to it, a face to it. We knew what it was, so at least we knew we had a problem we could solve. We had no choice—if she was to close on her condo and not lose the $30,000 she'd put down, we had to find a solution. At the time, I was naïve enough to think it could be solved.

This is when I needed Renée's never-say-die attitude—and she came through. She was a force of nature. She oversaw the hiring of the forensic accountant who went through our books. She found and met with a factoring company who agreed to front us the money, which we would pay back by turning our receivables over to them. We decided to cut back on phone services and to rent out a desk in our office for more income. We were moving forward—we were going to have this thing resolved and over—quickly.

We tried to pick things back up knowing this was just a small blip on the radar. Renée, Larry and I all took a trip together to Virginia to go to her sister's art show. We were still traveling for our clients. In May, I went to St. Martin for a client as part of their annual conference in the Caribbean and, as usual, my entire family came down for an extra week's vacation—and this time Renée joined us. On these trips, I always got incredible deals on hotels so my dad and his wife, my mom and her husband, my sister and her family and occasionally Lisa and Karl would come down and join us. It became a reunion of sorts and having Renée there just made it all the more fun. We thought that we had dodged a bullet and were no worse for the wear—but life doesn't work out that way, does it?

We went to pay off the $106,000 debt in full when the IRS informed us they had calculated wrong—we actually owed $111,000 and needed a new check. The factoring company decided that they couldn't really work with our business and did not want to assist us further. It is a testament to the people that we are that we did not take that $106,000 check and cash it. It was made out to our company. We had it in our hands, we could have cashed it, given it to the IRS, borrowed the other $5,000 and told the factoring company it was too late, but we didn't. We gave it back to them. To their credit, one of them really believed in us and continued to work with us to at least try to get us the money. Renée met with him and his partners, talked with them, tried to explain how our business ran and how we got paid and eventually we got the check, but they made it clear this was all they would do—which was fine. We thought it was all that we needed.

A month after we returned from our vacation the IRS informed us that we still owed over $130,000. And that was when my private doubts and resentment came in. I began to get secretly angry with Renée. She had found this loser accountant. As a matter of fact, she found him because he was the accountant for an account that she managed—who still owed us money. Why in the hell did we hire him?! Wasn't that a sign? He never got the other client to pay us! She was the one working with him on a daily basis. I started thinking that this was a result of her being too soft, too sweet, too accommodating; it was a result of her too often giving someone the benefit of the doubt. Renée was not one to confront people, so I felt that had she called the accountant on the carpet when this was going on, we wouldn't be in this situation.

I thank God to this day that these thoughts were fleeting and that I had the good sense to turn the mirror on myself. Where the hell was I? I was living my life, being married. I didn't want to deal with the accountant. I had never wanted to deal with the accountant. I was bad at math in high school and did whatever I could to avoid numbers. I willingly let it fall in her lap. I willingly let her handle the extra workload, the bills, the books, all while she had all of those accounts. I realized that I had let her drown under all of that. She could not possibly handle all of that and—oh, by the way, run the office.

Things were starting to crack at the seams. Our office was falling apart; one employee quit and two others were showing bad attitudes that we didn't know how to address. We kept trying to justify everything—they were young; we were young when we started; maybe we didn't give them the support they needed; maybe they learned from us. It was like working in a psych ward.

And I had been married only three months by now, and had to tell my husband we could possibly go bankrupt. That the IRS could take everything away, that after all of our hard work, we may have to start from zero. And to make matters worse, we couldn't do anything because we did not know what the IRS was going to do to us. I actually had moments where I thought it might be better to divorce Larry to protect his assets. I didn't want him to have to pay for something Renée and I had gotten ourselves into years before.

This is when his cool demeanor came in handy. Larry never worried. He never blamed me. He just told me to do what I had to do to get my business back on track. When Renée and I eventually had to reduce our paychecks to pay off some of the bills, he made up the difference. My family kicked in. Deirdre would front us our payroll and we'd pay her back when the money came in, usually a few days later. Mom and Larry lent us the money for rent, and God bless our landlords, Windsor Management. After explaining what was happening they told us to just try to pay something every month.

With that kind of support, we could not go down with the ship. Once, years before, Renée and I had had a big client who made up most of our monthly revenue (big mistake) who was starting to go out of business. We would call and call and beg and ask for our money, not only the money he owed us for work, but the money we had incurred on his behalf with FedEx, which was now in the thousands of dollars. Bill collectors were calling us, FedEx was threatening to put an ad in the paper to come and sell our furniture to pay off the debt and we were calling the client. Finally we looked at each other and we knew. We knew that either we were going to keep calling this man or we were going to go out and get new business and survive, and that's what we did.

And I think once we got that second notice from the IRS, we were at that point. Renée and I always said we were different sides of the same coin. We had different ways of doing things, but when push came to shove we were pretty much always on the same side of the fence. I think that instinct to survive kicked in. That friendship that we had built since the day we met at CNBC kicked in, that undeniable love and trust that we had in each other kicked in. People always used to wonder at how we did it. How we ran a demanding business, how we ran a company of all women, how we did all of that and still stayed friends. With all the madness and fear and moments of doubt that I had during this time period, I ultimately knew in my heart that Renée and I had an unshakeable love and trust in each other. We didn't try to work together, we just did. Maybe it was the way we initially started—she worked on her business and I worked on mine—that allowed us the freedom to not be in each others' hair. This was one of those sink-or-swim things, put-all-your-cards-on-the-table moments, and as we had done in the past, we just automatically started working it out—together.

We knew that one person had to focus on getting us out of the mess with the IRS and it had to be Renée. She lived in New York and it made sense. She had to be the one to deal with the IRS, to hire the attorneys (one to deal with the IRS and one to sue the old accountant) and the new accountant and the bookkeeper. And she was masterful. She lived at the IRS. She humanized us. She convinced them that we weren't criminals; we were just criminally stupid! She got them to hear us and hear our story. Fortunately we had a history of paying the IRS for the six years we had been in business before all of this happened, so we had a record of payment with them. Fortunately we showed our intent by paying the $111,000 in full. So they were willing to waive some penalties and fees and we were able to enter into a payment plan with them. I would come up and help her pull all of the paperwork together for her meetings with the various parties, the accountant, the attorney, the IRS, but one person had to be the keeper of all files—and that was her.

Although I was often in New York, my days were numbered. Larry was tired of me always being on the road and then also having to be in New York. We knew that our staff had to have more accountability for their actions and their attitudes. We were down to four of us with a full-time freelancer. We met with them to try to get the attitude in check; but we also had to be willing to give them more flexibility so that they would feel they could make decisions on their own without always having to consult with us. We agreed to impose a hiring freeze because we couldn't afford another dime on the payroll, but we also agreed to hire freelancers to help out as needed. We also went back to the little things, bringing in flowers, paying for MetroCards, closing early when we could and once in a rare while throwing in a massage for employees after a good event.

And we had to make our new roles clear to our clients: they couldn't always rely on me or Renée for things—they had a team working on their account and they had to learn to deal with and trust the team. We had started neglecting the financial health of our company because we were devoting too much time to making sure everyone else's business and projects were a success. We had to stop immediately. That process started taking some of the day-to-day management off our backs.

We started to focus on our business. What accounts were bringing in money? What accounts weren't? Renée had the philosophy of holding on to everything because at least it was money. I had the philosophy of letting smaller things go to make room for bigger business. Renée agreed that we could let some accounts go and I agreed to hold on to some accounts that I felt weren't generating the revenue. We started meeting regularly. It was agreed that I would come into town once a month to go over business. It was agreed that we would conference once a week about business. We also eventually agreed to get help procuring business. Renée had a college friend who worked on securing contracts. It sounds like an easy process, but for a small business you don't often have time to do the paperwork, the registering online and the follow-up. So we hired her to help us get registered with these companies and to join supplier organizations.

And I became focused on closing my deals. When this whole craziness started, I had some contracts that were still pending since before I had gotten married. I made it my mission to seal these accounts. I started to feel empowered again. I started to see that this could be my contribution. I would work to find accounts that would bring us some stability. I could also assist the office by handling some of the larger writing assignments that needed to be turned around. From writing the majority of the company's new business proposals to developing strategies and PR plans and writing press releases, I would be the go-to person. Ideas and writing always came naturally to me. Plus, since I could control my environment more than the office could, I had the time and the quiet to focus on things. I could also help organize things. I couldn't meet with the attorneys and the accountants, but I could get our office in order, our files, our records, make sure we were up-to-date on our policies and insurance. I could oversee the newsletter and deal with the production and the printing. I could be the lead with the procurement officer so Renée could deal with the day-to-day office procedures and management, payroll, staff issues and banking.

We are still figuring the process out, what works, what doesn't work. Some of the methods we discovered are recent lightbulbs. We still don't have all the answers, but in almost losing our business to the IRS, I found myself. I found that I had value and that I could contribute—in my way. Renée and I started to look back and be proud again of what we had accomplished and to not take it for granted. Within a year after the incident, we were back on our payroll system; we had a payment plan with the IRS; our bills were current and most of our old creditors paid off; we were able to give an employee a raise; we were able to put ourselves back on salary. We were able to do all of this with the same money that our old accountant said we didn't have. We started thinking about our future. We weren't young girls in our twenties who had years to figure it out. We were staring at the door of retirement and needed to put a plan into action. We started a 401(k) plan for our company. Personally, I started planning for my and Larry's future and working on our retirement planning. We got rid of our debt—all of it. I now pay my credit cards off in full for the most part. And although I am embarrassed at what I still find to purchase on them, at least they are soon paid off. We had narrowly avoided hitting the iceberg and I wanted to do everything I could to make up for the damage. Savings became tantamount, planning became tantamount, surviving became tantamount.

To be honest, we are still working our way through this, but the difference is, we know we are going to get through this—we *are* getting through this. My marriage remains intact and Renée and I came out stronger than ever—as friends and as business partners. We look out for each other more—and for our employees. We try to respect that they work hard and give us everything they've got when they come in the door, so that when they need time off or need to come in late, we give it to them. We don't rush anymore when people we've never heard of call us on the phone and insist we have to work with them and that we do a proposal *now*. If it fits into our schedule and the money fits and it won't cause us to change who we are and our style of working, then we'll do it; if not we'll pass. Even Renée is giving herself a little time off. Some of it was forced but she's no longer fighting it. I think she's realizing that it's okay to let go, to relax and to enjoy life. I on the other hand am learning that I can't rely on others to control my destiny. I was so good at being in charge and somewhere along the way I lost it. Did it start with my insecurities at CNBC when I felt like I had no idea what I was doing? Did it start with the bad dates and the feeling that no one was out there who "got me"? Wherever it started, that is irrelevant. I have been getting my confidence back, realizing that, yeah, I can have the kind of life that I want, but that I have to show up. I have to earn it. I have to do my part—and not compare my part to anyone else's part. I have to be fine with it all, to take responsibility for my role in where I am—I have to be fine with—and accept—and love—*me*!

I would not say that we are a super successful business, but we sure are a business that's successful at surviving. We are in a business that is allowing us to live the lifestyle we want to live in the way we want to live it. I pray at night to God to not bring me any business that's going to disturb this groove, that's going to disrupt this way of life that I want to live. I don't want to work with anyone who's going to compromise the lifestyle that I want for me and Renée and our employees—one of work, but work balanced with freedom, with flexibility and with fun. I know that that will be the key to our super success.

I know that we have to continue to do our due diligence for our business; that we are responsible for its success. I know that we have to take care of each other, to look out for each other; that I have to be "my sister's keeper"; that we have to call each other out when we're going down the wrong path, not hold it in with the hope that it'll correct itself. That it's an ongoing and continual process; that we have to stand up and be accounted for and stand up to succeed.

Renée

"Renée, you shouldn't think about buying a home as a single woman," said my mother.

"But, it doesn't make sense at all to continue to pay rent and not own a home," I replied.

"But purchasing a home is something you want to do with your husband. And, if you buy a condo or a home now, just what will you do when you get married?"

"Well, as I search for my Mr. Right, I'm just throwing away money. I've paid more than $2,000 a month to rent in New York City for years, and I have nothing to show for it. I think it is imperative that I own something," I replied sternly.

We went back and forth for another thirty minutes on the phone. This was a personal goal of mine—home ownership.

In a very traditional southern home like where I was raised, it was nearly a sin for a woman to live by herself, let alone own her own home. I had made my choice and this was something that I wanted to do and accomplish in this decade—my thirties. In my twenties, my parents had been hell-bent on me not starting my company because they thought that it would be too difficult and it would lack the security of working at corporation like CNBC—although people were fired there every day. Also in my twenties, when I wanted to move to New York City, my parents wondered why anyone in their right mind would want to move to "that dirty, grimy, fast-paced rat race."

I did. I thought it was the best city in the world. It offered me everything that Great Bridge did not. Ironically, I love where I grew up—Great Bridge will always be in my heart. It was and is my foundation. I long for the easy days of running in the fresh air with no worries . . . or with worries about picking pecans off the tree or shucking corn. On stressful days in New York City, I close my eyes and think of my pets, friends and family back home. But I guess it's just that I am a mixture of yesterday and today. I have married the two together. I wanted to own my business, my destiny, as my father had done, and own my own home. My parents didn't see it that way. They thought that I had to be married to be successful and own a home with my husband. But what if I didn't find my "soul mate" for another year, two or, even worse, ten? While my father thinks I'm too independent, my mom laughs because, she says, I am my father's child.

I hated defying my parents, but their advice was just that. My wings had to be extended beyond the traditional. I understood their concern and even flirted with it a bit myself; however, I knew that I needed to purchase a home or be left behind as the interest rates were at an all-time low—under 5 percent. I was in pursuit of my perfect home—a home that I could afford. As my lease was about to expire, in December 2002, I decided to investigate housing prices. The New York housing market was one to be reckoned with. There were one-bedroom condominiums that were selling from a half million to nearly a million dollars. I could not afford that. I wanted to stay in Manhattan as any single girl would. Brooklyn, Queens, the Bronx and Long Island were truly not an option.

Harlem was on the rise. Gentrification was taking place all over Harlem and I belonged to a church in the area, Abyssinian Baptist Church. I thought, why not Harlem—it would be easier for me to go to church and the homes were cheaper there as many New Yorkers were not aware of the beautiful architecture, larger homes and cheaper prices. I looked day in and day out. At the same time, my younger brother, Andrew, who worked internationally, suggested that if I had not found the perfect place by the end of the year, I could live in his place while he was still abroad. I needed something by May.

December came and I had not found the perfect home, but I felt confident that I would soon. I placed all of my furniture in storage, packed enough clothes to last three or four months and moved in with Andrew. This was really perfect; I could save additional money and pay off some of those dreaded credit cards. During the search for my new abode, I embarked on a program for first-time home buyers. This government program paid your closing costs, and no down payment was required—rather, you had to have a down payment, but they would give it back to you at closing. As a purchaser, you had to attend classes on home ownership and have good credit and a stable job. This was perfect—I was buying a home and saving money all at the same time. I would have my dream—home ownership.

Well, I got all of my papers in order. Everything they asked for. I made copies after copies. There were a few hiccups along the way. The manager of the program was leery of how there was always cash (a hundred dollars here or a hundred dollars there) coming into my account. I explained to her that I taught at New York University and often spoke or took writing assignments. They were so used to people just making one paycheck. Now, I thought it would be a positive that I was working hard to have additional income to purchase a home. For some reason, she just didn't seem to like me or she just wanted to make my life miserable. I stayed focused—the program would help me to save money and purchase a home. I must have faxed them my paperwork a hundred times. Each time, she would lose it. There were other requirements as well. You could not purchase a home for more than $300,000 with this program—this is difficult in New York City. Because it was a national program, I don't think the cost-of-living adjustment was made appropriately. But I searched and searched to find a home to meet the qualifications. I found a lovely townhome at $305,000, and asked the manager of the program, could I just provide the $5,000 differential. She said, "No!" Later I found another home; this one was $295,000, brand-new construction, doorman building, balcony and a great location. She told me that the building wasn't approved by them. Time for me was running out and I was striking out. The only saving grace was my real estate broker, Sheilisa McNeal. Sheilisa was one of my best friends and guardian angels.

God brings people into your life for a reason. Sheilisa kept by my side, finding condo after condo in my price range. One day, she found a condo that was just blocks from my church (she and I both serve on the usher board together). It was a two-bedroom in a nice neighborhood—everything in New York is block specific. This block was perfect. Now, this apartment didn't have a doorman, washer and dryer or parking (as I had in my last apartment), but it had two bedrooms and was in my price range. I decided that I had to make a choice. The apartment even needed some work. The seller was eager to sell as her deal had just fallen through and she had moved out of the condo to New Jersey. So I made an offer and she accepted. It was a done deal and I was well on my way. Or so I thought. I told my brother, Andrew, I was moving out. I set a closing date and I hired the painters for my new home. I had plans to redo this home—from the kitchen to the bedrooms.

Sheilisa provided me with a lawyer, one of her college friends. Everything was set. We had a closing date, I had given more than thirty thousand dollars down on the condo (which the agency promised that I would get back at closing), my brother's apartment was rented and in sixty days I would be moving to my first home! I didn't have the entire down payment, but one of my closest and dearest friends lent me the money—after all, we would get it back at the closing. I promised that right after closing, I would write my friend a check. Life could not be better. Everything at Noelle-Elaine was going well, we had a solid list of clients, I was dating the love of my life (or so I thought) and I would be moving into my first condo. Although the condo didn't have every feature that I wanted, I had come to love it. Sheilisa and I would go by and look at it. I had fallen in love with my new place.

Daily I would place X marks on my calendar to closing. One evening—not just any evening, the evening before I was to close on my new place—I received a call from my attorney.

"Renée, we're all set for tomorrow morning," she said.

I'm ready too, I thought to myself. I had even decided what to wear.

"There's just one thing," she said sternly. "I noticed a lien against your name, but I'm assuming it is not you."

"What do you mean a lien?" I asked with hesitation.

"There is a judgment against you for not paying taxes. We have an address at Fifty-one West Forty-second Street," she said.

"Our offices used to be there," I added.

"Let me call you back." she said.

By this time, my mind was racing a hundred miles an hour. I have always paid my taxes, what was she talking about? She called back and we figured it was for the company and somehow listed under my name *only*. Not the company name, not Kirsten and Renée, just that I personally owed more than $100,000. How could this be? She told me that we couldn't close and she needed to hang up again to notify the other lawyer and the bank that the closing needed to be postponed because of an emergency. This would give us time to figure everything out. I was devastated. I was sitting in my car, unable to move. It was getting darker and darker. I sat for almost thirty minutes, stuck on those words. "We will not be closing tomorrow."

I called Kirsten and together we figured it was taxes that the company owed that were not filed by our accountant. We knew that we had back taxes and our accountant had told us that he was filing.

The next days, weeks and months have almost become a blur. I needed to go full-speed ahead to get to the bottom of the situation, as the seller was not having this. She had gone through a bad deal prior to ours and was just fed up. She told my lawyer that we had to close within fourteen days or she was keeping my down payment—a down payment that wasn't mine! The program that I was going through thought that I was lying and dropped me. This was a program to assist those who do not currently own a home and was supposed to help you through the process, but instead they pushed me away. I tried telling them that we were unaware.

Kirsten and I later found out that our accountant filed nearly every tax return late and we received penalties and interest with each filing. When I called the tax help line and they pulled up our file, they informed me that our accountant had made many errors, errors that an accountant student would not do. What would I do? I now had no place to move to or live as I had already rented my brother's place. Luckily I have two brothers. My older brother, Lewis, suggested I come live with him and his family in Long Island until I figured the whole mess out. So I packed up my suitcases and moved in with him, my sister-in-law and best friend, Lisa, and my niece, Arielle, and nephew, Marshall. I felt like a homeless person—moving from place to place. There was no time to place blame. While Kirsten and I wanted to yell at our accountant, I found no time for that. We were in a pickle, a situation that overwhelmed me. It was *crazy*. Some people have asked me since that time, was I frustrated that the whole mess was on me. At that time, I couldn't think of that. It was just something that needed to be fixed and if I focused on blaming and why me, then I could not fix it. Kirsten has asked our current accountant why it was just placed on me. His response was that it's just random. He even noted that on many of the documents Kirsten's name is first as it was in alphabetical order. But I didn't have time to ponder such trivial questions—I was living a nightmare and wanted to make this dream better.

While all of this was going on, I had to go to work each day and put a smile on my face. One of my favorite songs is "This little light of mine, I'm going to let it shine . . ." It's a simple church song, but I would hum it each day, because while the seller insisted she would keep my down payment, I had no place to live, we owed the U.S. government more than $100,000 . . . I still had a reason to smile—I had my health and my wits. Sometimes things just go from bad to worse, but you must keep your chin up. While at Lewis's home, I was sleeping in the basement, and I tripped over one of the kids' toys and broke my toe. Now I was on crutches. I didn't realize that my toe was broken initially, so I walked on it for two days and it began to swell and fall to one side. It was summer, so I had on sandals, and a gentleman in a corner store said to me, "Excuse me, miss—how did you break your toe?" I said, "It's not broken. I just hurt it." He suggested that I go to the hospital. I did and the X-ray confirmed that it was broken. I was so preoccupied that I had not realized the pain or the hobble. To make matters worse, my car brakes died and those too needed to be fixed. More money.

There was just so much going on. I had always worked overtime, but now I was working twenty hours a day, as I was working with the IRS from nine until four; mixing in clients and additional client work after hours and had to drive an hour and fifteen minutes to Long Island to my temporary home in the suburbs. It's fine when you are coming home at six or seven o'clock. But I was coming home at midnight, sometimes two or three in the morning. I can't even outline my day clearly now. I'm not even sure how I managed. I was still trying to get new clients, maintain the old ones, manage employees, pay bills without having money—speak with the old accountant, collect all old files, find new people to review our books . . . oh, and not get paid because we needed to pay off the IRS.

Well, we hired a new accountant, Richard Levychin, who reviewed all of our books and informed us that there may have been other improprieties by our former accountant. During this time, we didn't tell our accountant that we suspected him of fraud and misconduct, as we still needed to get our files from him. This new accountant billed us more to get our books in order—not that we could afford to pay one dollar. He was billing us to get the job done. Each day, I was trying to figure out where could we get the money. I called friends and clients alike (this happened to be over the Fourth of July weekend, so no one in Manhattan would even pick up the phone), asking, "Could Kirsten and I have a loan for $100,000?" I know that sounds a little crazy now, but I knew Kirsten and I could pay it back. My goal was not only not to lose the more than $30,000 that the seller said she would take. There was even more at stake—I would still have to pay one of my dearest friends back the $30,000 and I would still have no place to live! This appeared to be a no-win situation—but I knew there was a way out. My dad always said you have to have faith and that is what I had. I prayed every second. Although things looked bleak, I knew deep down I had the fortitude for our business to survive. It wasn't just words that I uttered to myself, but words that I lived by. Dad always said, "You can do anything, just stop and think about it." I often say to clients, employees and friends, "Let me sleep on it." My father always said that, and today I utter the same words because a clear head is always better.

I figured that I needed to go to the IRS myself and explain. We had no knowledge of the situation. While that seems a little unbelievable now, it was the case then. Kirsten and I always focused on the clients and our product. We provided the clients excellent service and believed that the vendors we hired provided us great service. We allowed our accountant to be our savior. While he was initially responsible for our accounting, we then allowed him to be responsible for paying our bills. He would give me a stack of checks and I would sign them. I assumed if I signed them that he would send them off on time. That was not the case. It's so simple now. While we did not always have money to pay our taxes on time, he should have known that we should file them. Hindsight is twenty-twenty. He became a Svengali to us, giving us advice, paying bills—we trusted him with everything. We would often call him our uncle as he was older and we thought wiser. The ironic part about this is that we had been in business since 1993 and had paid our taxes and bills and managed everything well ourselves until we hired him. We hired him in 2000 and that was nearly our destruction. Looking back at our books and errors with the U.S. government, all of our problems escalated in 2000 and lasted until 2004 when we fired him. And he had the nerve to say we owed him money for the last two months before we fired him.

We made many mistakes with our old accountant, but the biggest mistake Kirsten and I made was to listen to him when he told us that we did not need to use our payroll service. We had used this service from nearly the beginning and had no problems with the IRS. But he assured us that we could save money by allowing him to cut our employee checks and he would know when we had money. If we had only kept using the services of Paychex, we would not have had so many of these problems. When I speak to small businesses now, I say, "You must have Paychex or ADP." It is impossible to survive without this or a similar service. Again, we listened to bad advice! And you can't go back. It's easy to see now how to avoid this pitfall. You can dwell and dwell on how you could see this or that, but then nothing gets done. That's why I did not, but instead I marched down to the IRS, just off of Forty-sixth Street in Manhattan, and asked for the officer assigned to our case, and her manager. I sat down, explained the situation that I was closing on a home and could not, as I had a lien against me for the company. It was not a personal lien but a company lien, and now that we were aware, we would pay it back in installments. She said that it was not possible, that they could not lift the lien unless the full amount was paid. The house could not be purchased without the removal of the lien. At that very moment, a sharp pain hit my chest; I started to hyperventilate and cry all at the same time. This was very rare for me, as I believed professional women should not cry, but I could not hold it in. What was I to do? Was I defeated? We owed more than $100,000. I had no place to live, no home. The seller would keep my $30,000. I owed one of my dearest friends, my heart, nearly $30,000. I had to pay it back, as I had given my word. And my friend didn't know anything different; my friend thought the money was sitting safely in the bank as it was planned. The guilt I had. I was on crutches with a broken toe. My employees needed to be paid. I was suffocated. I felt alone and no one knew what I was really going through. Although I would speak to Kirsten and she was my business partner and one of my dearest friends, I felt it was different for her; she was married and could rely on the strength and shoulder of her husband. I had no one. Ironically, I was dating someone at the time but we ultimately were on different planes. He had no *clue.* He knew something was going on, but not the devastation that my world was closing around me. And if he could not see this, then he could not be the person I thought. He was not the rock that I had imagined and anticipated. I often said that it is so easy for someone to be your friend when things are "good." Just prior to this pitfall, Kirsten and I had celebrated a decade of being in business with a gathering of friends, family and clients. People flew in to commemorate it with us; it was glorious. I believe destiny can always turn on a dime, and our destiny had turned. Now our company was shaky—I didn't know who to turn to. Although I have a strong, strong family and several dear friends, no one could help as they did not have $100,000 to give Kirsten and me at a moment's notice—and how could we dare ask? And as the IRS said, they weren't releasing the lien off of me.

I was just a number to them. I felt like a deadbeat and they just assumed that I was lying. Lying is an ugly trait. My father says the only thing you have is your word—so lying is not an option for me.

By this time, the manager of the department had come into the office. I felt I was having a heart attack as this moment; he took pity on me and said to calm down. I'm not sure to this day if it was because he was afraid that I was going to have a heart attack in the office or he just felt sorry for me. He assured me that he would work with us. He extended the time we could get the money—but I still had no money. I eventually left the IRS in hopes that I would think of something.

A lightbulb went off inside my head: we had a client, a friend, who was an accountant. I called him, and he came to the rescue. Richard Levychin was God sent. He suggested we go to an associate of his, Rafael Martinez, president of Republic Capital, which assists businesses by factoring their future income. The clock was ticking. I needed to have this done in days. I gathered all the paperwork he needed, traveled to his New Jersey office and back to his New York office and the deal was made. Things seemed to be coming together, or so I thought. His backers didn't understand our business, as this is typically done for companies who have a product to sell and not a service. We were not a viable client for them. His board would not approve us. Rafael believed in us and that we would pay the money back and he fought for us. I stressed to him, I gave him my word, and I begged him—please! It wasn't about pride; I laid everything out on the table. How Kirsten and I got into this situation. My question was simple: could he help us? I think Rafael understood. He was a family man, his wife worked alongside him—he could see that I needed help.

The clock was still ticking. I was calling Rafael every hour. I was calling the IRS every hour, I was calling my real estate agent—"Please, please, let her know that we are working on it and the lien will be removed." At the same time, I was still servicing my clients, managing our office, teaching at NYU and trying to keep a smile on my face. I knew that God would never give me too much to bear and he would carry me through this as a stronger person. People have more to bear than this, I kept telling myself. I knew that I could pull through, however difficult. I never mentioned any of this to my parents; I felt, why make them sad. I knew they did not have $100,000 to give me. My father would often call me during this difficult time and say, "You don't sound like yourself." I would just say things were tough at work. As my mother and I speak nearly every day, I believe she knew something was wrong, but she couldn't put her finger on it. I kept the conversations short. But just hearing Mom's voice made me feel better! People kept asking, "What's the holdup? Why aren't you closing?" I would just shrug my shoulders and tell them I was too busy and I should be closing soon.

IRS senior supervisor Evaristo Urbaez and I had made an appointment; I was to bring the check. Our accountant was able to get some of the penalties and interest dropped. I think once Mr. Urbaez got to know me, he realized that Kirsten and I had no clue, because once we found out about the debt we acted on it immediately. Rafael had the check made out and I was to pick it up at his New York City office. I did, but when I got to the IRS I found out they had made the check out to the wrong party. My deadline was here; I called Rafael on his cell phone and he had to issue us another check. The trouble was that the banks were closing in an hour. Again, this was a weekend and New York City on summer weekends is a ghost town. I managed to reach him and he said he would meet me on the corner where the IRS is located. I ran downstairs with another IRS agent accompanying me so I could get back upstairs (the IRS closes at four) and we began the process. The IRS gave me an official letter saying they released the lien and I did not owe any money. This was a weight off of my head because everything kept pointing to the fact that I personally owed this money. Now, for the next year, Kirsten and I were to pay

Republic Capital back. We had to manage our company with half the amount and still pay our bills. We took a reduction in pay. In fact, one payroll, we had to put it on our credit cards. We didn't receive pay often. The small reserve that I had from living at my brother's home while looking for a place to live paid off as I had paid off all my credit cards and managed to save a few dollars.

The IRS faxed the letter to the bank and I took a copy with me. I immediately called my lawyer and confirmed with her that I could close the next day. And we closed! Fate is funny; I managed to move into my new home and pay back my friend the $30,000 within eight months. This was longer than planned, but I was a woman of my word and I was determined to pay it back (working additional jobs and cutting back on my spending). Kirsten and I paid Rafael's company back as well. We thought we were back on track. But as fate would have it, not yet. We found out that while we had paid the debt to the IRS back, we owed another $130,000. We incorporated the company in 2002, while still under the old accountant. The IRS people informed us of this during one of my many visits to their offices.

However, it wasn't something that we had to take care of ASAP like before. So this time, I didn't feel the same pressure of a heart attack as before. We just had to figure out how we could do it. We set up a monthly payment plan. This seemed to take much too long. We waged a plan and the plan included acquiring a loan from Chase bank. It's all in knowing your banker. We had been told by other banks that it wasn't feasible, but our banker, who I would speak with all the time, Conrad Moy, managed to work it out that we would get a loan. So, today, the IRS has been paid back and the entire ugly ordeal is behind us. I am thankful for those who stuck by me and believed that our business could survive and believed in us. This was just a bump on our road to success. No one's life is perfect and the hard times only add to one's character, to their makeup. This was truly a dramatic chapter in our business, but it has made us strong businesswomen and even stronger people. If you let bad things stop you, then good things will never happen. I still have a great deal to learn and I'm still looking for my soul mate to share the good and bad times with. . . .

Chapter 10

The Aftermath: Going On after a Crisis

Renée

Can you recover after an economic and emotional crisis?
A resounding yes!

After September 11, 2001, New York recovered, America recovered—we were strong as a people. Crisis may hit each of us differently; however, it is our inner strength that allows us to continue on and persevere to create more successes.

> *I will lift up mine eyes unto the hills, from whence cometh my help.*
>
> —PSALM 121:1

Kirsten and I had made it; we evolved into true businesswomen. We had conquered misfortune and were on the mend and creating a dream company. Because I kept my inner circle small, there were very few people who knew the true story of our difficulties. It would not have been good public relations for our business if we could not manage the inner workings. It would not have mattered that we had an incompetent sheep of an accountant. Well, what's important today is that we got past our misfortune and turned it into a lesson that we will never live again. Yet we have decided to share our story for others to learn from our vast mistakes.

It's true: you can never "let them see you sweat." Whoever the "them" is—it's true. While we were pulling off the movie of a lifetime, we were now approaching the sequel where we had to take our company to the next level—and we did. Kirsten and I buckled down and managed the day-to-day operations; we managed the cash flow, our employees and ourselves. This was an easy task as we were on a mission to see our company succeed once again. We implemented new strategies, since we now no longer had the crutch of the slithering snake who we thought was managing our expenses. Our dysfunction was gone, we relied on ourselves for everything—we took control.

It was almost refreshing in a way. There was a sense of relief in knowing the IRS would no longer be hunting us down, this debt was paid and we had the power to succeed. We had empowered ourselves to manage us.

Ironically, the accountant had told us on numerous occasions that our firm was not making enough money to pay ourselves, the employees and all of our expenses. Kirsten and I sacrificed our salaries so that our employees could receive their salaries. We went back to eating peanut butter and bread.

The accountant was oh so wrong. On the contrary, today we make roughly the same amount and we pay ourselves, the employees and all of our bills. And we have created a 401(k) plan in which we match our employees' contributions, we offer health insurance to staff, we provide transportation through MetroCards, we have a savings plan in place. . . .

We learned that we could no longer keep our heads in the sand. While we love writing scripts, creating dynamic programs, developing strategic media plans and producing videos and shows—we always have to manage our business. Today it is still difficult, but we just remind ourselves how we can never go back to the black hole of no return. This challenge is extremely difficult for a small business because you never have enough time or energy.

Chapter 11

Despite everything we went through, we never had to file Chapter 11. So we will skip it here too.

Chapter 12

Final Chapter: Life Goes On

Kirsten

The tax thing was a sobering experience—one we are still learning from and one from which we are still feeling repercussions. While we are definitely in better shape financially, we are still suffering from the consequences of our carelessness and our former accountant's deceit and malpractice. We consider it a valuable lesson that we hope never to have to repeat.

At times we still feel like we are walking on a tightrope, but we are definitely looking toward the future—and the future involves change, which you can't always prepare for.

In March 2007, Danielle Grassi, our vice president and beloved employee of twelve years, informed us that she had accepted a job in California. Danielle was an integral part of our team and our success. She started with us as an intern and stayed and grew with us. We learned a lot together, we grew up together and she always believed in us—even when we didn't see eye to eye. She would always joke that she was the "dash" in Noelle-Elaine—and she truly was. She knew how to balance my personality with Renée's and, more important, how to manage the media relations, the event management and the production. Because she started with us when we were in one room, she absorbed everything we knew and that has served her and us well.

Of course no one stays around forever, and we knew that she had to move on to find her personal peace, but it was still a hard thing to hear, even if it was the right thing. But a funny thing happened after she left—the office kicked into high gear. During Danielle's last two weeks, we informed the clients, interviewed new candidates, held training classes for employees to make sure they were up to speed and even extended offers. Danielle held pep talks with the team, assuring them that they could do it without her, that they were ready for the next step and that she had faith in them. She even held our clients' hands, participating on client calls until the last day.

We had a great big party for her at a penthouse restaurant/bar, where a lot of our current and former interns and employees came to say good-bye. Even my mother and sister came as Danielle was like family and they watched her grow over the years. And the next day we all fell into place and did not miss a step.

I actually believe that our team rose to the occasion and broke out of their own personal fears and limitations to reveal what type of people they really were—and I don't think that would have happened had Danielle not left. Just as she needed to grow, we needed to grow and to know that we could survive change—even major change. Employees who feared production were now calling shows, writing scripts and creating rundowns, instead of observing someone else doing it. Quiet employees came into their own, holding client and team meetings. Everyone brought their "A" game. And the biggest test was when we did each event for the first time without Danielle and they all went off without a hitch.

We cannot thank Danielle enough for the years and the time that she gave to us. We are all still in touch with her and see her when we are on the same side of the country. But the biggest gift she left us was a prepared team with renewed faith in themselves.

And you have to have faith that you can grow and rebuild and succeed regardless of the circumstances. You have to continue shifting your model to fit where you are in life—life is always changing and we've had to make changes along with it.

One of our biggest changes is looking for that next generation of leaders to guide our company. Renée and I built Noelle-Elaine from the ground up, and we are proud of that, but our lives are changing. We are getting older and we no longer want to do the day-to-day management of running the business. Our work is extremely service oriented and as owner/operators we have been very much involved in the "service" of it all. I remember when I was on an alumni panel with businessman and NBA great David Bing, and he said, "So many small business owners are owner/operators and you want to get out of that." He was so right.

I am a wife and a businesswoman, trying to be a mother, and Renée is a businesswoman trying to live her life—we no longer desire to be on every call, oversee every meeting or attend every event. So at this phase we looking for our "heirs apparent"—people who will lead NE into the next phase; people who our clients will trust and respect; people we can trust and respect and who trust and respect us; people to carry out our vision and improve upon it in their own way. We have a great team in place now who we believe can fulfill that need—but it's up to them to decide if they want that responsibility. And it's our responsibility to make sure they are prepared and feel supported in their decisions; to allow them to make the mistakes that are so crucial to their growth; to let them be free to become the great managers we need them to be and that we know they can be.

But you also learn that you can't make everybody happy—not employees, not clients. Not everyone or everything is going to be the right fit; you can't prepare and predict everything, so you have to learn not to panic but to embrace change. Renée and I have learned that when push comes to shove, we have had to be able to do it all ourselves. That no one can be worth compromising our standards for; that the way we do things might not be right for everyone, but it's right for us. We have to balance that with being open to new ideas and new ways of doing things. And at times, we've had to get beyond our own egos to fight for an employee we think is worth fighting for—even if they do something that really upsets us. It's a delicate balance that we walk, sometimes more successfully than other times—but we walk it!

As for me—my focus has changed. You are no longer going to get me on the phone too much after five or on the weekends unless I am working an event or it is an emergency. I still cop to working late at times—just not talking with clients late! I got tired of feeling that I had to work seventy hours a week to prove myself, and I don't want my employees to try to meet that standard either. How in the heck did that become the standard anyway?! I have learned to accept that I am good at what I do and it's okay to know that. I have the years and the experience and I don't have to do a call at 8:00 p.m. or wait two hours for a one-hour meeting to prove that I am good or that I want the business. And my employees are honest and fun and dedicated, but that does not mean clients can be rude to them, think they are at their beck and call or expect them to work crazy hours because the client is not organized.

I have learned that the great clients are the ones who respect you and hear you out—who allow you the opportunity to go beyond even your own expectations and thank you for a job well done. I have learned that a good client is one who challenges you and pushes you to the next level without breaking you down. I have learned that those clients are invaluable and worth going the extra mile for.

I have learned that a good employee shares your vision and respects you, but always finds a way to improve upon what you teach them; that a nice employee doesn't necessarily mean a great employee; that the person you might think is right for the job may not view things the same way; and that the person you are most worried about can become your best employee—regardless, they all teach you something as you hopefully teach them. I guess that is the surprise and irony of life.

I've learned to adjust my style—that being a "yeller" shows nothing but a lack of control; that you can get the same results with a more balanced approached. On the flip side, I have learned that trying to be too nice gets you nothing but taken advantage of. At times I've felt as if I've lost my own opinions, trying so hard to be balanced and fair; I've have to relearn how to express myself, to be honest without putting a PR spin on something, to remember to be truthful and not tell someone—client, employee or friend—what I think they want to hear but what I believe is true. And that some people will get it—and others won't.

I have learned that sometimes friends don't want to hear the truth and I have to be fine with that. I have learned that others will never understand what I do and blame the shift in our dynamics on my friendship with Renée as opposed to understanding that we were building a business and *had* to work twenty hours a day together and it had nothing to do with them.

I've learned that true friends are truly happy for your success—and that you may be surprised at who those friends are!

But I have also learned that clients and employees can do well without me—and that is a good thing. In part of my quest to become pregnant over the years, I have had to give up some things. I have done the artificial insemination (three times) and in vitro fertilization (two times). I've been to the gynecologist, reproductive endocrinologist and the naturopathic doctor. I've been at doctor's appointments at 6:00 a.m., given myself shots in the stomach until I was bruised and had my husband give me three-inch needles in my back (thank goodness for ice). I have canceled trips because of procedures, taken ten pills a day, day and night—you name it and I have tried it. But doing all of that has made me realize that I have to slow down. I had to give up going to Nigeria and Tanzania for client projects (Tanzania being a trip I really, really wanted to go on), because I could not have the medicine in my system should I get pregnant.

At times I've felt like I have been "waiting for Godot," as I am still not pregnant, but I have also realized that the show would go on without me. I am getting what I have been hoping for—the office being able to operate without me and the clients starting to be fine without me. And with that I had to let go of my ego. You always want to feel needed and necessary and I had to accept the fact that at times I was neither—and that was fine!!! Everyone has been learning to do in my stead. We have had amazing projects go off without a hitch without my on-site involvement and each one gets me closer to my dreams—of being a great and fun wife and mom, of writing on the beach, of having a successful business that doesn't need our monitoring, of continuing to be creative, of having time to do what I want to do when I want to do it.

I am most proud of the fact that Renée and I have done this and are still continuing to do it. People ask how we have done it and are skeptical that we have never fought. Sure, we have had disagreements, sometimes major ones, but we always figure out a way to compromise and to work out a solution that we can both live with. Sometimes it goes more my way, sometimes hers—but we always figure it out. I think working with her and being friends with her prepared me for marriage. I know the two of us are unstoppable and I cannot wait to see what the future holds for us!

I am finding that the older I get the less responsible I want to be. I want to be free to work as I please, when I please and how I please. For once I want someone to recognize our talents as a company without us constantly having to prove it all over again year after year. I want to spend time doing nothing or everything. I want to sit back and read my *More, Pink, O, Black Enterprise* and *Essence* magazines and read about women who get it right. I want to read my *Cottage Living* and *Country Home* and *House Beautiful* and plan my house. I want to spend my time talking to women and letting them know that if we could survive all that we've been through and love it just the same, then they can do it too. I want to tell our story to the world because I think you always hear about the big guy, but rarely the little ones out there, day in and day out, cutting a piece of the pie out for themselves—maybe they can learn from our mistakes and not be so hard on themselves when they make them.

But I always remember to be grateful for the experience—for the bosses, employers, clients and coworkers who taught us so many lessons. To my husband and family for their undying belief, patience and love, and to Renée, who allowed me to become all that I knew I could be.

Renée

While it's important to understand basic business principles to run a small business, it is even more important to understand yourself; love, happiness and the acceptance of the choices you've made. Just don't take life too seriously—there's more to it than work.

My niece, Arielle, loves the American Girl store (the dolls, books, cafe and anything and everything about it), and one day while visiting the store with her and my sister-in-law, Lisa, I picked up a book called *Coconut's Guide to Life.* This book was perfect.

While it has only about fifteen pages with two sentences per page, I just loved it. I had to have this book, so I purchased it.

The book now sits in my office because the concepts are some of my life's lessons. It takes you back to being six years old. It would be great if what we learned early on applied to business today. Like: Listen with your head and heart. It's important to be a good listener. Everyone makes a mistake; apologize when necessary; be yourself. . . . It goes on and on with those basic principles for success. On the last two pages, Coconut tells us: "You're never too little to dream big dreams and a true friend stays by your side." Kirsten and I have had big dreams and still continue to dream.

Our initial dream was to start a business; we have done that and are successful. I've traveled the world, interviewed presidents of countries and corporations, and celebrities—all while remaining true to myself. We've learned to be adaptable and flexible in business. We've learned lessons that have allowed us to run our business for more than fifteen years. We've had ups and downs, or as I often say, there has been some pepper sprinkled throughout my life, and I would not have it any other way. I am thankful for my life as it is and all who have shared it with me: the good and the bad.

Because the peanut butter and bread sandwiches were well worth it.

I have been sidetracked a few times. But I remain steadfast on who I am and will always direct myself back to the main road. Kirsten and I have remained by each other's sides through thick and thin and we know that we can live our dreams.

And we have to live them today, as tomorrow is never promised to us. When we were in our teens and twenties it often seemed as if we were invincible. Or, at least when things happened, we were able to bounce back because we were not aware of all the complications.

Recently, I had to go to the doctor's office and was informed that I had to undergo surgeries, which led to a life-or-death situation at the hospital.

I'm *here* to say, life is too short and we must do everything we want to *now*. That as America changes and the world around us as we once knew it evolves, so has my life.

The lessons that I learned are very simple and I try to live by them each day. I've followed *Coconut's Guide to Life* and the basics of the Ten Commandments from the Bible. Whether you are Christian or not, these commandments allow for an orderly existence with your fellow man/woman. While I can't say I will never lie in my life—you know there's always that "little white lie"—I can say that I won't be judgmental about others as I once was.

In the Bible it says "He that is without sin among you, let him first cast a stone. . . . "

Who am I to say my "little white lie" is not as devastating as another person's sin. It's all sin.

In the spirit of who I am and who I would like to be—I can only be true to myself and, as such, enjoy life and hopefully leave an indelible mark to inspire someone else to pursue their dreams and make a difference.

Not putting off that vacation, spending the extra time with a loved one or sharing my life with someone, because you and I will never know our last day.

Live life *today* as Coconut would.

As for my current dream, I hope to find someone to share my life with and become my great love and eternal soul mate. As I hope to live another forty or fifty years, I reckon I have a whole lot of life before me and I hope that includes a husband, children and fulfilling additional goals such as giving back even more to the America that has offered me so very much.

Kirsten and I plan to continue to give back—whether it's training homeless women to become professionals, creating scholarships for needy kids or simply giving Easter baskets to poor kids.

My journey for happiness continues.

A Final Thank-You

We would not be who we are without the current and past employees who dedicated their time to helping us realize our dream, and for that we will be eternally grateful:

Angela Altus
Kelly Beaty
Stephanie Clark
Lisa Donadio
Lisa Douglas
Tiffany Foxworth
Sitella Glenn
Danielle Grassi
Carol Johnson Green
Linda Harding
Chris Hayes
Mandy Karangelen

Michelle Lamb
Ron Magas
Takita Mason
Danielle Maximo
Quamiesh McNeal
Jim Murray
Michelle Pascal
Patriennah Acosta Pelle
April Prince
Donna Stewart
Vera Vathi
Derrin Woodhouse

We'd also like to thank the hundreds of volunteers and freelancers over the years who have been our extended arms and legs. You are too many to name, but you are all in our hearts.

Thank you for letting us learn and grow and make mistakes with you!!!